CW00552486

Throughout her childhood, Simran was made to feel that she had no worth in her family and was treated with indifference and cruelty.

One day, her father announced that they had found someone in India who was prepared to marry her. She refused, and left home.

Simran knew how angry her family would be. They would also be ashamed: by refusing to marry a suitable man and "running away", she had brought great dishonour on her parents.

Her disappearance would be kept secret for as long as possible, but sooner or later the rest of the clan would find out and the shame would escalate.

"Your father says you are no longer his daughter."

To Nabila, I share my story
with you in hope of friendship
and honesty, that we both deserve,
in a world where secrets of misplaced
honour or shame are useless.
— Best wishes & Love from!
Jasvinder Glen
— Simran K.

Simran was disowned and rejected by her family for
making her own choices for her life.

By sharing her journey of pain and healing, she hopes to
help others, showing that family is not just about flesh
and blood and that there is hope for victims of prejudice.

There is hope.

CHILDREN OF HOPE

A Survivor's Story

by Simran Kahani

Published by Filament Publishing Ltd
16, Croydon Road, Waddon,
Croydon, Surrey, CR0 4PA UK
Telephone +44 (0)20 8688 2598
Fax +44 (0)20 7183 7186
info@filamentpublishing.com
www.filamentpublishing.com

© Simran Kahani 2012

Printed by Berforts Group - Stevenage and Hastings
Distributed by Gardners

ISBN 978-1-908691-17-0

The right of Simran Kahani to be identified as the author of
this work has been asserted by her in accordance with
the Designs and Copyright Act 1988

All rights reserved. No portion of this book may be used or
reproduced in any manner without the prior written
permission of the publisher.

Inspired by real events.
Names of people and places have been changed
to protect identities.

Contents

To my 'Children of Hope', Ami and Adam,
who know the good aspects of their heritage.

To Philip, who has loved me unconditionally.

Prologue

It takes me a while to notice that there are tears streaming down my face. I touch my cheeks with my fingers, but they are so wet that I have to use my hands to wipe the tears away. I am crying uncontrollably, yet there is no sound coming from me. As a child I was taught not to show emotion; it was seen as a sign of weakness, something to be ashamed of or ridiculed for. My mind is blank, it is the only way I can cope and keep my composure. I am crying for the person lying in the pine coffin which has been placed at the front of the crematorium hall, a person I loved despite everything that happened between us.

I have been shown to the back benches of the crematorium; it is almost full. There must be several hundred people squeezed in, solemnly paying their respects. As we wait in silence for the service to begin, I look over the heads of proud Sikh men in white turbans and respectable Sikh women in white chunnis and search the crowd for familiar faces. The bereaved family is sitting at the front with their backs to me. One of them turns around: it is my aunt, who we called Bhabhi as children – she was always interested in young people and seemed a warm person from her hugs and smiles for us. When she sees me, she stands up and comes over, telling me to come forward and sit with the family. She is an understanding Sikh woman and knows that it is easier to grieve and accept that someone has died if you see their face and say goodbye. I hesitate. Just as I am about to do as she has suggested, I recognise my mother, three sisters and brother – they take a brief look at me then turn away. They show no sign of wanting me to join them, in fact it is clear I am not welcome to sit with them. My aunt shakes her head sadly and leaves me standing at the back of the hall.

I am still in shock, having only recently received the call from my brother telling me the news and warning me that if I want to attend the funeral I must come alone, without the one person who has cared for me for the past few years – my husband. The coffin starts to move slowly along the conveyor belt; there is an odd click, a turn, then no more is heard. My chest is tight and my heart is beating so hard I can hear the blood pulsing in my ears. My mind is full of questions to which I fear I will never get the answers. What happened? What were the circumstances of his death? Who was there when it all happened? I try to recall what my brother told me when he called to break the news. Then my knees buckle as I remember what he said before he put the phone down.

"It's your fault," he said. "You killed him."

It is my father's funeral.

Chapter 1

A History Left Behind

"The past is a foreign country: they do things differently there."
(L. P. Hartley)

My parents, who the family called Mamaji and Papaji, were born in the Punjab, North West India, during the early 1920s into a community known as the 'Tharkhans'. Such communities were defined by the occupations they held. Tharkhans were blacksmiths and carpenters, as opposed to 'Jhats', for instance, who were farmers and landowners. They were ingenious people, producing some of the finest tools and furniture for miles around. Later, in England, my father would marvel at the carpentry of Queen Anne legs on tables and chairs, and go on to reproduce some beautiful handcrafted pieces of his own.

I know my parents' history through having listened to them talking to others, or between themselves; it was never something that was told to me. I was fascinated by this aural history. They lived their later lives reflecting on the past, as for them it had great meaning for both present and future generations. It was an aural rather than a written history. I know little of my parents' actual day to day lives as children in the villages of the Punjab, but I do know the names of the villages they came from, in a region of Punjab, known as district Jullundar. These were places leading off the famous GT (Grand Trunk) Road running from Delhi through to Punjab and across the north of India.

My mother was a small woman of strong build, no more than 4'9" tall. I like to remember her with her long wavy hair (which she usually kept tied up), her full lips and smile. As early as I can recall, she would talk of her hard life in the Punjab with her family, as a young woman milking cows, churning butter, cutting corn which she then had to grind to make flour, doing endless jobs for her many siblings – eight boys for whom she had to wash, cook and clean. She had a sister who died early, leaving just herself and her mother to manage the household. Her mother, my grandmother, was blind from birth – I do not recall meeting her, although in the photographs I saw, she was a tall, thin woman, nothing like my mother. Mamaji often told me that their relationship was strained at times, presumably due to the pressures and hardships of their daily lives. She would tell me and my siblings that she had never been allowed to go to school and regretted not having had this experience. I could not imagine not being able to go to school, as school was the making of me, but my mother not being allowed to go gave me an insight into how dependent her family was on her for their survival. As if to make up for this, she became skilled at embroidery (dasothi), cooking, and not least in reading the Sikh scriptures in Gurmukhi (the sacred written language of the Sikhs) all self-taught; by looking and asking questions, she had pieced together her own education. My mother knew that the way for a woman to excel was to learn and recite the Sikh scriptures and to be the best cook and seamstress. Still, despite these extraordinary abilities, she seemed to lack confidence in herself. I would watch her around people when we were out at family events; she would shyly look at people, sizing up what they were saying, sometimes with an uncertain smile. I recall her telling me that when she was a young girl, she wore a gagri – a large flowing skirt down to her ankles. Mamaji had her nose pierced as a young woman, as was the culture for girls at the time of her growing up. She had her ears pierced and the lobes of these were very long as she had worn earrings from an early age. She would love to sing traditional Punjabi folk songs, and listen to Mohammed Rafi and Lata Mangeshkar songs from the old movies that I love to this day. I thought that she looked like Lata Mangeshkar, especially with her full lips and smile. She wore a long and heavy gold necklace made of solid gold in the shape of peas and diamonds, giving this beautiful jewellery the name 'Matar Mala'. It was a gift from my father and she wore this every day, from the earlier days of their marriage right through to her ageing years. This reflected against her dark brown skin, glistening with the beauty of a time and fashion past, but not lost to my mother's memory.

My mother reflected upon her early life with sadness, for she had experienced the loss of many people and was uprooted from all that was familiar to her on several occasions. She was raised to respect and serve men – not only by cooking and cleaning for them but also by practicing 'purdah', meaning that a woman had to have her head (and sometimes her face) covered at all times in front of men. She always had to put them and the family first and was not supposed to be outspoken. However, I also recall when I was a child that she was rarely lost for words within our family setting and amongst women from the extended family. On occasions when she felt strongly about something, it seemed as though the harsh realities of her life could not stop her giving her opinion. Given that her life had been quite hard, I think she sometimes felt misunderstood. Opinions were often within the realm of what she was taught and had experienced in terms of right or wrong: modesty, for instance, was important. Mamaji was a follower more than a leader, her frame of reference always the experience of family life and religious values and instruction.

The women in these close, extended families were often thrown together. Whilst they delighted in the traditions of weddings and often talked about the latest fashions, they also learnt to support each other. This mutual emotional support was not unusual for me to see when we went to visit family and friends, and Mamaji seemed to need this – she would talk openly about the hardships in her life with other women in her age group, who knew what she had experienced. These women were prepared for marriage from childhood: you knew from as early as you could understand that a groom would be found for you. Choice was not in the realms of my mother's world, nor was it a matter for any women in her clan to question; it was a set part of life itself, to be accepted as something your parents would do for you, supposedly with everyone's best interests at heart.

In fact, all decisions were made by the family as a whole, but predominantly by men; they were involved in the running of the household and decisions about money, betrothals and many other things. Obedience, acceptance and submission were the virtues that women were supposed to possess; this was the way for a woman to earn respect, essential for the 'Izzat' (pride/honour) of the family, but in particular that of the males.

My mother was betrothed to my father when she was ten and he was several years younger; they had been promised to each other by their families from an early age. My parents' families were part of the same clan, Ramgharias who were part of the Tharkhan caste. Members of this community would take the issue of marriage very seriously, exchanging information about potential brides and grooms in order to ensure the best match for the families concerned. Often, a child's marriage partner would be decided at the time of its birth, if not before. Otherwise, a third person called a 'bachula' would be called in to act as the 'middleman' (or woman), bringing together two families whose children were a potential match. This is how my parents' marriage would have been arranged – it is how things were done in 1930s India, and is sometimes still done by families the world over today. However, my parents did not actually live together until they were officially married when my father was eighteen years old. My mother then moved to my father's village, where he had been building a large house for the future family – a house that I went on to live in during the early 1960s. It was here that my mother and father would make plans with my paternal grandfather to move to East Africa. I have little knowledge of how all this happened, but I do know that this was a major event for both my parents. For my mother, everything she had known was about to disappear, everything would be left behind to start a new life, not only with a new family but also in a new country. She would spend a lifetime going back in her mind to her village, her brothers and the rest of her family.

My father was a strikingly good-looking man of average height, around 5'7". He had a fair complexion, strong, open eyes and a huge smile. He wore a turban which always looked well starched and was cleverly made, so that when he took it off, it sat stiffly on the table like a hat. The turban represented his respectability and his faith as a Sikh. He wore white turbans mostly, although as a young man he did wear different colours.

My father's village was the place belonging to people who held his surname: not all, but most of his relatives would have been from the same village. To my father, his village was where his tribal roots were. He was a proud man who held the traditions and values of his community in high esteem, but it was not unknown for him to question some of these, often laughing at some long done away with custom. For instance, I recall people – both men and women – kneeling to touch my father's feet out of respect because he was a more senior and esteemed figure to them. He would smile or laugh, raise them from the floor and tell them that they did not need to do this. He was embarrassed. However, at times he would be expected to do the same to someone who was his senior.

I know little of my father's early life. I know that he was fluent in Farsi, Urdu and Hindi Gujarati, as well as his mother tongue, Punjabi. He spoke some English but understood more. He must have had some education because he also wrote Punjabi and Urdu. I was fascinated with my father's ability to learn these languages, some of which were very different despite their linguistic connections. I know he would have learnt the craft of carpentry and the blacksmith's trade from men in the family. He was also a builder, as the family home in his village was built by him and still stands tall and significant on a small, dirt track road. The house was made of cemented yellow walls. Some of my early years were spent living in that house, a house that he was proud to have built with the help of the men in the family. All the buildings including our own were basic and almost 'biblical', with stone steps moulded from cement leading to the upstairs courtyard; the craftsmanship that went into the details of the doorways and verandas will remain forever etched in my mind. It was a house that I was proud to be part of and to have lived in.

My father came from a very large family, a group of eleven or more siblings . This family was further extended by my paternal grandparents (who died before I was born), their grandchildren and even their grandchildren's children. It was a great source of amusement in the wider family how my sisters and I were the equivalent of 'great aunts' to some of the other children in the family who were not much younger than ourselves, which I never quite understood. To my father, the discussion, reflection and detail of his enormous extended family was the talk of nearly every conversation with visitors and anyone else who would listen. Because the Tharkhans (and later the Ramgharias, a clan that my family belonged to) were all somehow inter-related by marriage, nearly everyone we met was family for one reason or another. For anyone to step outside of this tight circle was unheard of. Certainly, marriage proposals had to remain within this clan.

My father's relationship with his brothers and their families was sacred, especially early on when he was growing up, but also later when he married. He spoke of little else. His faith in Sikhism was steadfast and unquestionable: this was his guiding influence when all else failed or when problems arose. He lived for the pilgrimage to Amritsar and the Golden Temple. He was a Sikh of the Five Ks wearing his Kaccha (shorts), a Kirpan (small sword) around his neck, a Kara (iron bracelet), and Kanga (comb). His Kesh (long hair, although he had little of it) was covered by his turban. He was also a traditionalist at heart, following the culture of his community, living in fear of his extended family and maintaining their honour through his actions and of those of his wife and children. All the major decisions that affected our immediate family had to be made with the extended family (and other notable people who had their trust) through discussion and consultation. Decisions about my family's future move to Africa was also made with them, as well as issues and problems about our livelihood, sustaining the family and most importantly, family honour. Nothing was allowed to escape their notice or could be decided without their input and agreement.

My father was about four years younger than my mother, although they would often quibble about this (she did not want people to know that she was older than him). He was a good-looking man and turned women's heads when he entered rooms, much to my mother's disapproval. She would never say it but she was uncomfortable on occasion with some of the women in the wider extended family who obviously favoured my father. Later I found out that he had had a desire to marry another woman, to the great regret of my mother. This indiscretion was well known to us since she told us all about it when we were children, and although my father happily took on the marriage with my mother as part and parcel of life, it played on my mother's mind even after his passing away, such was her pain. Apparently, he gave up this woman to his beloved brother. It would be this uncle and another relative, in later years, who would ask my father to disown me for the sake of the family's honour.

One major family event that happened in India before they moved to East Africa was my mother giving birth to a son. All I know about him is that he lived until he was two years old. I have little information about the cause of his death, but I vaguely remember tuberculosis being mentioned in later years. Understandably, my mother did not speak about this event very often, my father even less so, although I recall in my early life my mother crying many tears. The loss of this sibling saddened me and the thought of my parents losing a child also affected me. I felt for them. I went on to learn that my mother had many other children through miscarriage at various stages of pregnancy, either in Africa or India. This would have been very difficult for a woman in those days, since her value was based on her being able to bear healthy children – especially boys. Pity would have been unwelcome, but my mother must still have felt judged. It was only later I realised that medicine and good healthcare were not as easily available to women like my mother as they would have been to women in the west.

My parents' journey from India to East Africa may have been made in a ship called a dhow; almost certainly my paternal grandfather's was, as this was the way many people travelled in the 1940s from one continent to another. At the point of their departure there was much unrest in their homeland, the partition of Pakistan and India being the main concern. In the 1940s, factors such as British rule in India divided political views between different religious groups; the feudal and tribal functioning in villages of the Punjab and the poverty experienced made migration the only chance of a decent future for many. Punjabi Sikhs had migrated to East and Central Africa in the 1890s as artisans and railway men; many exercised the rights of colonial status to travel to East Africa again in the 1940s. My father was recruited to work on the East African railway which ran from Mombassa to Kampala. At this time my parents lived in Nairobi. My father's brothers and their families all lived together and worked for the railway board. My grandfather and his brothers also settled in East Africa. During these years the Second World War was making its presence known, while Martin Luther King, who was born when my parents were children in the 1920s, preached peaceful resistance and racial equality, a doctrine that was greatly influenced by the success of Mahatma Gandhi.

The Sikhs who united to establish their community in places like Nairobi, Eldoret, Kisumo, as well as places in Uganda such as Kampala and Mombassa, worked extraordinarily hard, building up their own communities and organisations and financing these themselves. Gurdwaras (Sikh places of worship), pharmacies, shops and Sikh schools were just a few of the structures that Sikhs built and maintained. The Ramgharias established their own community group named after a Sikh pioneer and a place called Ramgarh Fort. Their religious roots always remained the central focus of their activities. My parents first settled in Nairobi but moved to several places around Kenya and other parts of East Africa, whilst my father worked for the railways.

In Nairobi, my parents lived in communal units called 'Landia', where each family had a private area to themselves but shared dining and social facilities with other members of the group. My parents said that the years they spent in East Africa were some of the best times of their lives. Although they were, in effect, in exile from their own country, they saw this as a time of plenty, mostly a happy and stable period where they enjoyed a good climate and provision that they would never have seen back home in India. Whilst in Kenya, my siblings and I were born. My eldest sister Noor was born in 1953, followed by a second sister Jay and third sister Ambi before I arrived in 1959 and finally my brother Dev in 1962. My brother's birth at the end of our time in East Africa was to have a remarkable effect on both my parents and myself as the youngest female child. The birth of a boy was not only considered honourable, it was also significant for the care of parents and other members of the family into the future. Before my brother arrived, my parents were regularly reminded of their deficiency by people who felt sorry for them. When my brother was born, his birth was celebrated by my parents' relatives and friends with great joy.

I was born in Kisumu, which was a settlement next to Lake Victoria near Nairobi. Even now I am not sure whether I was born in a hospital or at home. My mother was in her forties at the time of my birth. 1959 was the year that the Austin Mini went on sale in Britain for £300. The first known human with HIV died in the Congo, Fidel Castro came to power in Cuba after a revolution created the first Communist state in the West, and Mattel's 'Barbie Doll' was launched. Harold Macmillan was Prime Minister of the United Kingdom. More importantly, the music at this time included great artists such as Buddy Holly and Cliff Richard; big musicals included *My Fair Lady* and *The Sound of Music*.

I remember little of our life in East Africa. Mamaji told me that I was cared for at home by her with the help of an 'Ayah', or mother's help. This ayah was Kenyan and spent many hours looking after me, apparently singing Christian songs and hymns around us children. I have often wondered about the significance of an ayah in my parents' lives at this time and in mine as a result. I am now touched and honoured that I was fortunate to have a Kenyan woman to play with me and care for me, and am aware of the sacrifice that she would have made to come away from her own family; however I also became acutely aware in my later years of the fact that Africans had the 'lower' jobs or no jobs at all in their own homeland, and that many Asians owned businesses or worked for the British in Africa. I also recall my parents expressing respect for African people as they were hardworking; many Kenyans were employed by Sikhs, Hindus and Muslims at this time.

I know that my two eldest sisters, Noor and Jay, were fairly close from the beginning and were renowned for their beauty and cleverness. They attended a school in Nairobi which was predominantly made up of Sikh children. My sisters excelled at everything they did. They had the assurance of their cultural and religious heritage and experienced a freer way of life in Africa in comparison to 1950s India. At this time, my sister Ambi would still have been too young to attend school.

Around the time of my second birthday, my mother took me and my siblings back to India. My eldest sister Noor would have been aged nine at this time and the youngest being under one. It was 1962 and by this time, my parents had lived in East Africa for almost eighteen years of their lives. My father, however, stayed behind, ostensibly because of work.

I recall the years that we spent in India as the saddest of my early life. I now believe that the events during this time affected all our later interactions as a family and the dynamics of our communication. I must have blocked out a great deal of it then, not least because I now know that I would have experienced being abandoned by my father and felt the lack of any bond with my mother. My mother's return to India alone surprises me now, because life was so hard there and she was very isolated. I was never told exactly why it happened but I suspect that things were not settled in Kenya, at least not politically. The African National Congress was rightfully influential in the lives of Blacks in South Africa and many Asians were dissatisfied with life in Kenya under Jomo Kenyatta. My father had returned to visit India on his own at some point within those eighteen years, but as work in India was difficult to find, he remained in Kenya.

In the Punjab, we returned to poverty: basic living, no toilet, only a stand up washroom with a concrete floor and a hole in the wall where the water would work its way out through small open gullies in the house until it went outside. The toilets were the fields on the edge of the village, where we women would go together in small groups. There was a water pump in the courtyard of the house downstairs, and the water had to be boiled and cooled before it could be drunk. Both the water and electricity supplies were temperamental, neither constant nor readily available. Clothes were washed by hand, and cleaning and dusting were ongoing, time-consuming activities. Our cooking area was a small corner room where we crouched down on bare feet by a fire, cooking in an oven made of bricks and clay. The house had a flat roof where we would dry clothes – as well as our hair – as we stood there on certain days in the sun. Still, despite these basic amenities the house was our pride, as it was built by my father and, in comparison to many, it had plenty of room.

The physical tasks involved in the caring of five children resulted not only in pressure on my mother but also in demands increasingly placed on the shoulders of my eldest sister Noor, herself still only a child. We struggled to obtain the food we needed (we grew vegetables but this would not have been enough), and shopping for the basics was an all-day event since the nearest towns, Guriya and Phagawara, were several miles away and could only be reached by oxen-drawn carts. Also, my mother's health began to deteriorate. She had been pregnant when she arrived back in India but had suffered another miscarriage which resulted in her having a hysterectomy, from which I believe she never fully recovered.

During these years, I recall some painful events. I missed my father and often, especially when my sisters beat me for things that I could never understand or remember having done, I would think about him and wonder if I would ever see him again. Nothing was ever explained about his absence. I used to go and stand at a railway crossing on the edge of a field, waiting for a train to come and imagining that my father would be on it, as I did not know how else he would return. Whenever the train arrived and he was not on it, I was always disappointed.

As the youngest female child, I seemed to be the scapegoat for all the family's problems. Often my confidence was badly knocked – I could never do anything right in my sisters' eyes. One day I was at school with twin girls about my age – five years old at the time. They were always dressed in fine, clean frocks and they had fair skin which was so valued by everyone whilst my own skin was dark, and not valued; it was not unknown for me to hear this remarked upon when my mother and siblings spoke about me. I recall playing for hours after school with the twins by a large pond called the 'Chapper', near to school. I didn't want to go home as I was enjoying playing with the girls, but eventually I had to return. I remember the escalating screams and a beating from my sister Noor on my return home. It was not enough to just slap me, which I was used to – there was hair pulling, dragging and general shouting at me. I recall to this day feeling numb and very frightened by the hands that were used to strike. I eventually learnt to cry for long periods to avoid further insults, sobbing alone for hours before going to sleep. Once, walking to the top of the Grand Trunk Road, I was suddenly confronted by a goat and was hurled in the air. There was a lot of blood, and although my memory of the event is vague, what is clear that I lay on my own beside the track in pain and terrified of what my sisters would do to me when they found out; anything to do with me was seen as a nuisance to them. I was eventually found by the family and taken to a hospital in one of the bigger districts of the Punjab for stitches to my head. Nothing was expressed; the job needed to stitch my head done as a practical matter, the trauma left for me to deal with. It was a huge event for me, the scar on my hairline a reminder of what was an insignificant event to my family.

Usually I was the last to learn of any family event that was going on. One day, I discovered that Noor and Jay were planning to hold a party in our walled garden, the plot of land where we grew vegetables, kept the cow for milking and stored dry cow dung for use as fuel for the fire. I was told to stay out of the way as I would be a nuisance to the guests. Of course, I hid behind the entrance to the garden and peeped through the iron gate. It was like looking through a window into another world, one beyond the tight confines of the village that I was used to. My sisters' teachers and friends wandered around the garden chattering and eating tiny chapattis and other food that was being cooked on the open fire. I was mesmerised; this was not a world that was ever shared or discussed with me, nor did I feel that my sisters cared enough about me to teach me about it. I wondered what it was like for them at their 'big school' in the larger town.

On another occasion I was suddenly sent to a nearby village, where my father's sister Pooha (meaning paternal aunt) lived. I was left there for many days and in this strange place I was very unhappy and could not understand why none of my siblings had come with me. When I returned home I felt as though I had been sent away because I was not wanted or needed by my family. A lot of these events were significant to me as I was often not informed of what was going to happen. I was left with a feeling of abandonment more often than not, with no real explanation provided in these situations. I clearly recall that my siblings had never been sent anywhere outside of our village, so this incident always felt very strange.

There was no expression of love or touch between us, which to me seemed particularly cold. I felt that my mother never really bonded with me and had very little time for me. I recall her relationship with all the others seeming more practical, especially with my older two sisters, although it was very different for my brother as the boy child.

Dev was treated like a king from the time he left my mother's womb. He was breastfed until he was four years old, which is difficult for me to believe now, although it may not have been unusual then. My mother's relationship with Dev was one of protection and support, keeping him close by her and feeding him with titbits such as crushed almonds. She always made sure he had special food and was served first. His clothes were a priority: nothing but the best would do. He was not expected to lift a finger. I would often look at his hands and notice how smooth and clean they were compared to the women's, which were red and dry from washing and cleaning. In fact, we were told that we should feel honoured to look after him and care for him. My mother would often show Dev off proudly so that people could give him the attention she felt he deserved. I knew that without this male child my mother would not hold the standing she did in the wider family and community. She had wanted a son for so long, but with this came a clear demarcation between the females in the household and my brother and father. Dev always knew that he was seen by my parents as the special one. We accepted this without jealousy, in many ways conforming to it because we knew it made our parents happy. The bonding between Dev and I was not allowed to happen physically – we rarely played together and he would be picked up if I sat with him for too long. I often felt sad that I could not be closer to him; we were only one year and nine months apart, and I longed to spend time with my little brother. In later life, the school that was chosen for him was not the one the girls attended – it was a better school, in a middle class area.

Because I was kept away from family discussion or any interaction with adults, I saw little of him, but I recall one incident when a male relative dangled me upside down from the top of our tall house from the flat roof, holding me by the legs, Michael Jackson style. I was petrified. I have not forgotten it to this day. This was, apparently, to evoke some feeling in my brother and it clearly did affect him, as when he was an adult he admitted that it was the only time he ever had any thoughts of concern for me.

Whereas my sisters could talk and do things together, I always felt pushed out. The negative image of myself that I was presented with by the family was of 'Kali' (dark skinned). I was ridiculed for this, and learnt early enough that dark skin was not acceptable to my family. I felt ashamed of my difference. I was a small child for my age: again this was seen as a problem, and ridicule played a part here. My hair was very curly and fussy, unlike my sisters who had straight hair or a slight wave; mine was especially curly and therefore difficult to plait. It was a dreaded chore for my older sisters, who would pull and tug at me and my hair whilst the plaits were being done, and I remember being fearful of being slapped if I moved in the slightest.

I began to take on the negative image which my siblings and my mother projected on to me. I didn't feel good about myself or valued as a person, and didn't feel that I had a place in the family. The beatings continued and so did my tears. I must have been crying as much for the physical punishments being meted out to me as for the affection I craved. The bruises and scratches were nothing compared to the emotional pain I was suffering.

These events are very marked in my mind; it was at these times that I most thought about and yearned for my father. His image was built up by the family as being the one who would come and sort out all our problems, and I believed he would sort out mine. But, as time went by, I almost gave up hope that he would ever return.

In fact, my father did visit us once in those years between 1962 and 1966. I know I was happy to see him, but there is a great blur of events round this time. However, I do remember that we went to Hazur Sahib, a famous Gurdwara. While we were all sleeping outside on the open marble floor around this place, a thief stole my father's wallet from under his clothes. Although clearly shocked, my father was a man who moved on and didn't let what happened affect him, unlike my mother who was always shaken by the dramas of life and became quite emotional. These events shaped me at a young age. I was a child who never had an explanation for anything, but instead learnt about the world through the joys and terrors of everyone around me.

My time at school – I was there for just over a year until I was six – was a strange experience. I stuck out like a sore thumb. I wasn't a happy child from the start, and our family was treated like ex-pats; people in the village felt we were different because we had come from East Africa and were being kept by my father from a distance. I learnt the Punjabi alphabet, however, and watched how maths could be taught to children with a stick whipped across the hand. The teacher was a large woman with a stern look. The classes of some forty or so children were taught in the open air; a basic building was available with nothing much inside it and we had to sit on the floor. The preferred style of teaching was simply reciting everything the teacher said, with no questions allowed. It was a government school with few resources, in fact the teacher was practically the only resource provided. On occasions, government schools received free milk powder in packets which we would dip our fingers into and lick as we walked home. This was a reminder to me of the poverty around the village. I remember, however, the heat and the long sunny days and being glad to sleep at the end of the day as children do when they have been busy learning about new things at school.

There was also an incident which upset my mother greatly. The villagers, like many in India, were highly superstitious. Even though it is not part of the Sikh faith, superstition would often be very real alongside religious faith, and many lived their lives under the influence of these thoughts, believing that if you washed your hair on the 'wrong day' or were not kind to someone, then some evil would befall you. One morning we were called into the garden where there was a great commotion going on. In front of the iron gates was a 'toona': bits of turmeric and red powder and burnt offerings of sorts, a kind of witchcraft which was meant to warn my family of some terrible thing. My mother was beside herself.

Although this wasn't fully understood by me, I felt upset for my family. My elder sisters could be rude to the neighbours and they were not liked by some of them. There was also jealousy because we were thought wealthier than most in the village; but really, our lives were no different to others – we still had to struggle like most of the people there.

I recall a very kind act by my mother: an old man with a long beard would come to the house most weeks and sit in the corner of the courtyard. He said little, and Mamaji would put food in front of him, some chapatti and dhal. This would be repeated regularly throughout our years in India. It did not occur to me until much later when I returned to India as an adult that this man was homeless and poor and was dependent on my mother to give him a meal whenever he was hungry. This was the generosity of Sikhs that I have so often seen, and it is considered a kind and Godly thing to do. Although my mother believed in reincarnation and that through doing good deeds, God would look on us favourably and give us better karma, for me the spirit in which she did these kind acts of generosity were selfless, as was the care of her own brothers.

I remember little of when and how arrangements were made for my mother and siblings to travel to England and join my father there. It must have been in 1966 when I was six or seven years old. One day there was a lot of upheaval in our store room downstairs with my sisters helping to wrap, pack and lock away things that were precious to my mother, such as pots and pans and furniture. I understood that we were going somewhere but thought that we would only be gone for a short time, returning at some point to the house and unpacking everything again.

My lasting memories of the Punjab of my childhood are green fields and the luscious vegetables that came from the surrounding farms: corn on the cob roasted on our open fire at home, tall, thick sugar cane stems which the farmer snapped for us to suck the juice out of, 'Sakar Keh' – raw sugar lumps melted in butter which we ate on chapattis when we were really hungry, 'Malai' – the cream from the top of cow's milk, and churned butter that we piled on top of hot 'Saag', a fresh spinach dish. I remember the big house with its green painted walls and the upstairs 'best room' where framed pictures of my father and grandfather hung proudly on the central wall for everyone to admire.

As we drove away from the house, I wondered, "Is Punjab where I belong? Or do I belong in Kenya? Or do I now belong with my father in England?" Where *did* I belong? We drove to the airport via the Grand Trunk Road wearing our best clothes, crisp and ironed, smelling of moth balls and sandalwood. Soon we arrived and were seated on the plane, and I had my first and most memorable journey in the skies.

Chapter 2

England 1966

"In my Father's house are many rooms; if it were not so, I would have told you. I am going there to prepare a place for you."

(John 14:2)

The journey from India by plane, although nauseous for some of us, was most memorable for me because it was the first time I saw a woman wearing a short skirt. As the air hostesses walked up and down the aisle, I was so shocked, I had to close my eyes. It was considered shameful for women to show their flesh in this way and I had never seen or known of women who could feel comfortable dressed like that, and I didn't know what stockings were either! We were all 'properly' covered up in traditional clothes, me, my sisters and my mother in our salwar kameez (traditional Punjabi dress).

The experience of flying would have been exciting for any seven year old, however the uncertainty of where we were going and what we were likely to find when we got there made the journey emotionally charged. All I could think of was that we were going to meet my father. Looking back, that scene from the film *The Railway Children* comes closest to this memory, where Bobbie is on the railway platform waiting for her father. He comes through the fog of the smoke and she runs to him... I was incredibly nervous, and it was hard to believe my mother when she said we would see our father again. My brother Dev was now four years old and my father would especially want to see his only son whom he hardly knew. We had all missed some of our formative years away from him.

On arrival at Heathrow, there was an emotional reunion. We approached Papaji who had some relatives with him. He lifted Dev up in his arms and then there was a hug for us all and, unusually, tears. Then he directed us and our luggage to the transit van which would take us to our new home in Handsworth, Birmingham. My first memories of England are sitting in the back of the van in the dark eating Genoa fruit cake which came wrapped in cellophane, our father talking to us, the night illuminated by the lights of a busy dual carriageway, of tiredness and wondering where I would sleep. It was dark and cold and we were on yet another journey, but we were with our Papaji.

"Where you goin' our kid?"

Preston Road banter is in full flow as I play on my own at the front of our house. Mrs. Maggie, as I know her from the kids down the street, thinks all the youngsters belong to her. I stand in front of her nervously: I am nine years old and I don't know what to say – I decide to run! I run as if she is going to catch me up, I am afraid of her as she is white and my world is not yet accustomed to being outside of the close circle of family and extended community, my heart is beating really fast. I don't know why I should feel this way. The reason I think I run like this is because we are told that 'goras', or white people, are to be kept at arm's length. Mamaji says, "Be careful! If goras speak to you, you must run away."

The message was clear from everyone at home and it was a message of fear: we don't have white friends, and life is separated between our home and the dangerous world out there. I don't know if my mother was afraid that we would be subjected to discrimination or worse, but it didn't help me to learn that this could be a safe world where Asians and whites lived together. I was allowed to go to the corner and penny shops to spend the odd coin I might be given to keep me quiet and I was occasionally allowed to play on the street outside our house on my own. Such freedoms were appreciated by me despite the fact that they were obviously to keep me out of the family's way rather than an attempt to help me adjust to my new world.

England and the culture outside of our home and family life was making its presence known through my sister Jay's pictures on the wall in the bedroom – Engelbert Humperdinck and Tom Jones torn from pop magazines – away from the eyes and ears of our parents. The four sisters shared the upstairs front bedroom, where the radio blasted out songs by artists such as Simon & Garfunkel.

Once, I had to go to the corner shop. On the way I saw a white woman on the doorstep of her house, speaking to me and holding out some money. She looked interesting to me, wearing a flowery pinny which many of the English women wore, and with a mass of rollers in her blonde hair. I didn't understand a word she was saying as my English was still no more than a few single words... "Hello", "Shop", "Yes", "No". She probably wanted me to buy her some milk from the shop or something, but instead of trusting this stranger as the other children playing on the road would have done, I was cautious and frightened, not a bad thing today, but in the context of families who were used to helping each other out, it must have seemed odd to the woman that I just stood and stared at her. When she threw salt over her shoulder I was even more afraid – was this the 'toona', the black magic that I saw in the Punjab outside our garden? When she did that I ran away from her as fast as I could: my heartbeat took a long time to return to normal! However, I soon realised that the two different worlds I now inhabited – home and the outside world as well as school – would have to be separated out if I was going to learn to live in my new environment and get to know people, which I very much wanted to do.

Benson Primary School in Winson Green was my first real experience of white people. When people in my community said the word 'gora', they always laughed. I didn't understand until later that 'gora' ('white man') or 'gori' ('white woman') could be used either seriously or jokingly. At school, my teachers were male and female. There were no male teachers at my school in the Punjab. I recall one male teacher, Mr. Corrigan, at Benson. He was American, as was his wife, and they both taught at the school. His wife would sometimes come into the classroom to ask what time he would be ready to leave. He would look at us and pull a face like a grizzly bear, go up to his wife at the classroom door and, in full view of the class of forty children, kiss her aggressively on the cheek and mouth, ending with a long, sucking noise. The whole class would erupt with laughter. Needless to say, this was my first introduction to anyone kissing and at that time I thought only white people kissed; also, in my community, any kind of physical touch between men and women was not allowed. I was shocked. Mr. Corrigan was one of my best teachers; I would see him with his wife at the bus stop right up until I finished secondary school. I thought he was wonderful but as a child of nine or ten, I was terrified of approaching him or his wife alone!

Some time after my family's move to England, a couple of years into us settling in Birmingham, my sister Noor got married. She was seventeen. Like most of the events in our family, I was not aware of what was going on until the last minute. I was by now very familiar with bedroom doors being closed in my face and being told to keep out. A few days before the wedding there was a flurry of activity – a lot of people were crowded into our small house; cooking went on around the clock and the smells even reached my bedroom late at night. The lounge became a vegetable cutting area and endless cups of tea and mithai (Indian sweets) were served to the men in the front room. Papaji was discrete; to celebrate, he drank beer or whisky, but only with people who were not as strict as the more religious members of his family, with whom he only drank tea. I had no issue with my father enjoying the odd drink because I knew how hard he worked in the steel factory. This was a constant struggle for him; with his extended family, it was always a hide and seek situation. I would see this many times, especially during the weddings of my sisters and brother. I saw by the way he paced up and down that it made him uncomfortable, and understood how complex his family was. Some Ramgharias eat meat and drink alcohol whilst the stricter sect of our family were practically vegan and teetotal.

I was confused about my sister Noor; she was marrying a boy from India who was apparently known to my family whilst they were living there. There was talk about him from our time back home. He was to be my 'Jija', or brother-in-law. Out of respect, we were expected to call him 'Bahji', which means 'brother'. I was also worried in some other strange way; up until now, Noor had been my main caregiver, bathing me and doing my plaits. Mamaji spent a lot of time either going out to chat with the neighbours or sleeping on the sofa. Noor managed the household cleaning. Whilst Mamaji might cook the 'sabji' (delicious vegetable dishes) for the day and on occasion wash clothes and hang them out, but for the most part, she left everything to my sisters. Jay, who was around fifteen by then, stuck solidly by Noor. Between them they were often to be feared for their matron-like running of the household, shouting at everyone to fetch this and that. Even my mother was afraid of them, usually saying little and never questioning their bullying tactics. My sister Jay had a difficult disposition, often getting so angry she would slap me and shout obscenities; this was not just for not helping with the housework or leaving shoes where they shouldn't be, but because bad moods would be taken out on anyone in the way. As the next one down in age from Noor, Jay would now be my caregiver. I wasn't looking forward to it one bit.

I was nine when Noor got married. At that time I was feeling very unsettled. I was in another country and still had so much to learn, especially at school where the new language was complicated, and things at home seemed far from well. As if to pass my cares on to Noor, after her wedding I was to be her escort on the coach taking her, her new husband and members of his family to their home town in Luton, a long way from Birmingham.

On the coach I sat with Noor and Bahji. She had her head and eyes down, a long pink bridal scarf pulled over her face. The decorative 'Gota' (ribbon) on her scarf was silver and sparkled in the sun coming through the coach windows. There was a smell of sandalwood about her; her young white hands were painted with mehndi and her nails with bright pink varnish. Bells on the 'Shakuntala' chains around her ankles jingled at the slightest movement. She crumpled a handkerchief in her hands, wet from the tears of a new bride being sent on her way to a new life with people she did not know. Her husband wore a turban, smiled, and had a glint in his eye. I was not sure if I could embrace him as my Jija yet, I didn't know him and neither really did Noor. My heart felt heavy for her. How could this be right? They had not courted, nor did they speak to each other like friends should speak. Would Noor be OK? I sat quietly for the whole journey. Noor and I were the only females on a coach of over 100 men, the usual drinkers worse for wear after the celebrations. It was an overpowering feeling of men triumphantly taking my sister away from her family so she could serve their own.

It was the summer holidays, school was out, and so I would be in Luton with Noor for at least five weeks after her wedding. There was just me, Noor and Bahji in a small terraced house. I had a bedroom to myself which was the first luxury I'd had in a long while. The house was immaculate; Bahji had been decorating and Noor had things in place, woe betide that I should move anything. It was a nice house but there was silence most of the time and no affection from Noor. She kept busy all day, washing clothes, cleaning, cooking and gardening. For the first time in many years she made me lots of pretty frocks on her sewing machine which I really liked and was touched that she had done this for me. However the tension in the house increased but I didn't know why. Noor put food in front of me but had nothing to say. We didn't know how to talk. I tried and failed but felt that without her, I would not be cared for, and lost. It was an incredibly lonely place for us both to be.

One day, Noor was very angry and shouted at me. I had eaten a lot of large juicy plums from a tree in the back garden and the juice had badly stained a dress she had made for me, as well as my skin. She asked me to strip and stand in a bowl in the garden whilst she scrubbed my knees so hard I thought they would bleed. It occurred to me that she was trying to scrub the dark pigmentation off them, not the stain. She did not like my dark colour; nor did my other sisters, Jay in particular. They reminded me often enough. Over the years, I realised that my being the darkest child in the family gave my mother and siblings reason to be angry with me. It is hard to believe that your flesh and blood can have such distaste for the colour of one of their own. It took me many, many years into my adult life to understand that this anger was about other things, not me, despite the direct taunts I often received about the colour of my skin.

I went to sleep that night lonely and sad. Why was I feeling Noor's sadness? What had happened to her to make her look so distant and alone?

In the morning she was on her sewing machine, as beautiful as ever in her hand sewn salwar kameez. But it was an almost clinical environment, not one I felt as a child I could disturb.

The five weeks went by mostly quietly, except we would have visitors in the evenings, the house would be busy and it was easy for my care to be neglected.

Around this time, I was sexually molested by a relative who came quite regularly to visit. I have chosen to be discreet about this issue in my memoir, to prevent identification, however he hugged me roughly into his armpit and smiled, saying in Punjabi, "That's good darling, you're going to have a bath." Then he slid his hands up and down my body, between my legs and private parts, for some time before letting me go. I made my way to the bathroom feeling confused about what had just happened. Was he showing affection? Was it right? It didn't feel as if it was. This continued throughout the holiday. He was clever about where this would happen, which could be anywhere around the house. I began to feel uncomfortable but could not tell Noor, as she would surely punish me. Would I feel the back of her heavy, strong hand, as I had so many times before? I was sure that I would, or did she know what was happening? She never talked to me, so how could I say anything? If I did, would it bring dishonour to her, to my family? Would I be punished by them all, including Jay who was closest to Noor?

As the days went on over that summer and while Bahji was at work, and Noor busy with sewing, I plodded around the house with nothing much to do. Then one afternoon Noor asked me to take some clothes to the bedroom where she and Bahji slept. When I put the clothes down, I noticed some magazines under the bed. Cautiously I bent down and picked them up to get a better look. They were pictures of naked women and I had never seen anything like these before; I put them back quickly, aware that it was wrong to see them. There were generally things in my environment that I would hear and see that I did not understand as I was only ten years old.

After these things happened, I became frightened of men around me and became very adept at escaping the particular relative's wandering hands. I think he knew, but he would still pass sly comments; I was never sure if he was addressing me or his feet. I felt sick at the thought of how he saw the women around him. I did not understand at this age that what he did to me was wrong, but the fear that I felt whilst I slept through my time in Luton, was unnerving – all this affected me deeply. The atmosphere was heavy, and I felt terribly sad and alone. Although I could not articulate why, I also felt very worried for Noor's new environment in this town.

When my parents and sisters came to pick me up, I was relieved to be going home, despite what might be waiting for me there now that Noor was no longer going to care for me. It was nice to see their faces so happy when they saw Noor. The matter of the relative remained buried until I was well into my late forties when my brother told me that complaints had been made about him by the Gurdwara with suggestions that he touched children inappropriately. He said that my father had been told and that he had had words with this relative. The rest I do not know. I felt proud of my father's integrity in dealing with this matter, even though it was never for me. All I remember through my teenage years at family events was me watching this relative's every move, because I did not trust him. He avoided my gaze because he knew what he had done, but it was clear that he took every opportunity to be negative about me and my choices. He made my life very difficult with the rest of the family; I often wondered if this was because he saw that I would speak out about injustice, and was not the subservient young woman that he and others believed that women should be. Ambi knew of this immense dislike of me by this man, and at times could empathise with the situation.

Top of the Pops was on telly and we did our best to get to watch it but when Papaji saw Pan's People for the first time, it became the first in a long list of programmes which were unquestionably forbidden. Unexpected kissing scenes in particular caused a great deal of embarrassment. There would be a direct order from Papaji to "turn it over" and we'd quickly do as he said; it seemed by the look in his eye that we should be ashamed, it was as though we girls had done something wrong. *Dixon of Dock Green* was acceptable and Papaji watched this with some respect. He saw a reasonable white police officer, not unlike his mates at the steel factory, doing a respectable job. He wanted to believe that white men upheld the law, and he found this the best way to look at the people who did appreciate and understand different communities. He loved the humour, the wink of the eye and the "Goodnight, all". Papaji had been in Britain since the early 1960s. He had seen Africa in turmoil and this was a new start, a new chance. He had worked for the British on the railways in Kenya and now he worked for the British in the steel factories in England.

Papaji's other favourite TV show was wrestling and Mick McManus. Every Saturday at 4pm my father would start going red in the face, getting more and more excited as Mick fought with his competitor. At every elbow drop, he would jump up and shout. You would think he was actually there, helping Mick do the job. Papaji was happiest either talking with the men in the family, playing with his grandchildren or sitting on the sofa with a

Guinness and Mick McManus. I could sit next to him then and nothing pleased me more. He would show affection on occasion; with a hand on my head, he'd say, "Go and get me a cup of tea, Beta" ('Beta' is an affectionate word for a child). He wouldn't look at me directly because of purdah – the invisible curtain between men and women, even father and daughter, where they talk but never look each other in the eye. I wanted Papaji to love me; in fact, I knew by his gentle hand on my head as a young child that he did. The other way he would express love was by buying us mithai from the local 'Halwai', the Punjabi sweet maker – hot Jalebis and Samosas, still in their warm brown bag.

Apart from these small gestures, love was not physically shown or emotionally expressed in our family and yet I longed for both because my experiences had been so cold and very lonely. I never saw my father much; sometimes I'd catch him at the end of the day after his long shift at the factory, often lasting twelve hours; he would return with a sooty face and dirty clothes and go straight for a bath, his food and then sleep. I felt for him; in the sixties and seventies, working in a steel factory was a hard, physical job. My father's earnings would not have been sufficient to properly feed and clothe us all, but what we had, we appreciated. There were no toys for us girls although I recall on one special occasion, relatives bought me a teddy and a tea set. Sometimes I would be allowed a few old pennies to go to the penny shop for plastic baby dolls and feeding bottles and the like. If I managed to squeeze a three penny piece I thought I had got really lucky! Play was not considered necessary or important and often my small gathering of toys would be thrown out by my over-clinical sisters without me even knowing until it was too late to get them back. Toys were of no real value, a waste of money. In any case, a portion of my father's earnings was always saved for my sisters' marriage dowries. If we wanted our own money, at the age of sixteen we could work in retail. Even then, my sisters had to save for their dowries. The fact that they were expected to provide for their arranged marriages was a constant worry to my parents, but it was an inevitability. Noor's had been done; now the pressure was on Jay. She was seventeen.

I began to resent things like not being able to go on school trips which were costly. I knew I shouldn't ask my father, but I so wanted to go and be part of the crowd. For days I would build up to the moment when I could speak to him about it, feeling anxious and guilty and not knowing what I should say. I wasn't used to direct communication with my parents; they existed for us to do things for them, not for us to ask them for things. This is how I felt. If I asked her for money, my mother would grumble and produce a small purse from the middle of her bosom and complain that she didn't have enough, my father hadn't given her anything. She was never confident about financial matters either. However, when they had it they would lavish money on my siblings, usually after their marriages; perhaps this was their way of showing affection.

I would always defend my father. To me, he could do nothing wrong. My mother would talk of their past and they would argue, shouting at one another. These arguments would tear at all of us, and often they were in the evenings; we siblings would go to bed listening to the voices downstairs – the tension was hard to break. I decided it was my mother who was wrong because she was not – in fact had never been – there for me; this was, in my mind, reason enough to side with my father. I said nothing but we siblings watched and felt the sadness. I did not fully understand what it was that my father had done but my mother had reasons, reasons I may never know. There are things best left unsaid about the accusations that my mother levied at my father; I never knew what to believe. Years later, I blamed my mother's depression and isolation and the loss of so many things in her life on my father but I also understood that I did not know enough about the things that my mother complained about. Perhaps she didn't tell us because she wanted to protect us. However I would go on to have compassion for my mother knowing what she had been through.

My final year at primary school was particularly hard. After Noor's departure, Jay took on the responsibility of cleaning the house, but she was never happy in her role. My mother had relied heavily on Noor, and Jay just wasn't cut out for this, her temperament was volatile. Any small thing could trigger an outburst of outrage. I was very frightened of her, as I would be hit if I was in her path.

I recall her beating me with a wooden shoe called a Scholl. This was something new. By the time I was due to go to secondary school, the slapping, taunts about my colour, abusive language and name-calling in front of Ambi and my brother Dev had escalated. Usually they were carried out away from my father but nearly always when my mother was around. Mamaji would occasionally say, "Leave her alone." With that, she would make a dramatic exit and head to a neighbour's house. I felt hugely let down by my mother; she never made any great effort to stop Jay's abuse, she did not protect me or place me behind her for safety. I never felt my mother's arms around me. Jay did not need many excuses to start the violence; we all lived in fear of her. She didn't target Ambi much, although she would moan and groan at her. Ambi stayed out of Jay's way. I knew that Ambi feared Jay's behaviour too from her dismissal of Jay and telling me that I needed to do the same. Jay would never say anything to Dev either; he was a boy and so that would be unheard of. He also knew that Mamaji would protect him; he was still allowed to sleep with my mother, and did so right up to his pre-teens. There were times when Dev and Ambi would watch these unnecessary beatings and look on silently, unable to express any emotion. Even so, I could tell from the look in their eyes that they knew this was not right, that someone should be stopping this from happening. I would have to remove myself for safety, going up to my room even though it was too early for bed. Usually I was too confused to sleep. I accepted the beatings as a normal thing but could not understand why I deserved such harsh punishment. Looking back now, I can still feel the injustice of all this, and have recognised this for what it was: wrong.

Ambi and Dev never sided with me; they saw my unhappiness as something that was my own fault. Dev would point out my size and dark skin and say I was not as attractive as my sisters. Ambi felt that I should pull my weight with housework: by the age of ten I would stand on a stool or chair to reach the sink as I was already washing my own clothes, cleaning dishes and making the chapatti dough, amongst other things. But it was clearly not enough. Still, despite the bullying, I felt sorry for Ambi as it was obvious to me that she was not happy either.

Chapter 3

Secrets

"There are no secrets better kept than the secrets that everybody guesses."

(George Bernard Shaw)

S eptember 1971 saw me in my navy blue school uniform: a below-the-knee skirt and white shirt with a blue-buttoned cardigan. On my first day at secondary school I walked in like an officer, so proud to be part of something, anything but home. I was determined to enjoy this new start: this was 'big school', I would finally be at school with Ambi, maybe she would protect me here. I was very proud of Ambi as my older sister; she was beautiful to me and underneath I thought that she had the potential to love.

This was a new beginning for me – in some ways school turned out to be more of a parent to me than I'd ever had at home. This 'parenting' initially came in the form of my class teacher, Pat, who immediately took me under her wing. She and the other teachers at school seemed to think I was cute, perhaps because I was a very small eleven year old, no more than about four foot tall. Pat was also my Religious Education and Music teacher. From the beginning she had a huge impact on me. I had never spoken intimately with an adult before and yet she singled me out and seemed to want to talk to me. My school had a population of Asian and Caribbean girls that represented at least eighty per cent of the total number of pupils attending.

My hopes that Ambi would protect me, however, were short-lived. Of course, she was there first, and when her little sister, me, ended up at the same school as her, it was as though an unwelcome awkwardness had besieged her. It wasn't long before the Sikh students in her class found out. They smirked and gave intimidating belittling smiles as my sister said something to me about straightening out my fresh school uniform. They were the big girls at this all girls' school, with their prefect badges and slightly modified navy blue and white uniform: Punjabi 'pyjamas' (tight legged trousers) underneath skirts, hair pulled back with little rebellious wisps around the ears, to go with the fashion of the 1960s. Ambi taught me well how this would be transformed as soon as we got home, hair tied back more neatly and flesh hurriedly covered up. However

Ambi was even more daring than me and I liked her look: she backcombed her hair and wore stockings under her above-the-knee skirt. She wore an elbow length polo top on which she pinned her shining prefect badge. I wanted to look like her, yet knew full well that my four foot nothing frame, neatly plaited hair and long, plain skirt were a far cry from the girl that I saw in my dreams. Ambi decided to ignore me at school and walked there and back without me. I was eleven, she was fifteen. I didn't understand why she didn't want to walk with me; and although by then I should have been familiar with my sister's distance from me, it still didn't stop me wondering why things always had to be that way.

A few months later, the secret came out. Some of the Asian girls in the year below Ambi's had recently been chanting, "Your sister's got a boyfriend," along with the usual embarrassing comments such as "slag" that were common to some of the working classes in Handsworth. I was not familiar with swearing, and when I learnt from my counterparts at school what these words meant, I wondered why they would want to say that about my sister. I loved Ambi, how could they say such things about her? I pushed it to the back of my mind, it was another thing that I was not old enough to understand.

There was a girl called Jagjeet at the school, and one day she was pestering me about Ambi.

"Ahh, your sister's gonna get in trouble. She's got a boyfriend!" she said in her thick Birmingham accent.

"What do you mean?" I asked, frowning.

Jagjeet laughed. "Go and see for yourself then, 'cos after school she walks down the alleys with that boy."

I could feel the heat in my face rising, wondering if this could be true. Ambi didn't want to see me at school, she didn't want to walk home with me and she avoided me in the house. I was uneasy all afternoon and more than forgetful in Science, not really concentrating. I decided to find out for myself on leaving school and followed Ambi home without her seeing me. I felt a bit shaky about doing this, but hoped that my friends at school would be proved totally wrong. As I crept up the long alley, or 'gully' as we used to call them, I saw Ambi. I stopped and held my breath. She was locked in a kiss with a boy who was wearing a white shirt, an Asian lad. I didn't recognise him but later found out that he was from the boys' school next door, behind the wall that separates the girls from the boys. It was all very quick. She looked up and saw me and instantly we both had tears in our eyes. She called out, "Don't tell..." and I said, "I won't!" I ran very quickly away from the gully, all the way home as fast as my legs would take me; just before I opened the front door I wiped away my tears and went upstairs as normal to change before Papaji came home, to hide the fact that I was wearing a skirt, just like Ambi.

Little did I know how much this would impact on my future life, my choices, my capacity to realise that choice was within my grasp. Ambi – my nearest role model – had been brave enough to make choices for herself, going against all my parents' values and doing everything that they would object to and punish her for, if they knew.

Ambi's relationship with me seemed to get better overnight. She began to listen to me and talk with me more. I was aware that she was always much more worried and cautious than I was. I would question the order of things, Ambi looked at the sad state of affairs in the lives of the family members. I felt she would accept things that were not good. I also felt that emotionally she needed the relationship with her boyfriend to cope with the lack of emotion in the family. I supported her in this relationship knowing that she hid and kept things quiet over many years. I would sometimes see her with her boyfriend, reminded every so often that this continued. It was a painful secret, one to be kept at all costs, both for myself and for Ambi.

During this time, at school I learnt to play a little guitar and was taught how to study the Bible and pray. I also grew close to my teacher Pat, as she would be there for me when things went wrong at home. I had formed an attachment to her, as if she was a surrogate mother, and so had many other girls in our group; we all competed for her attention. She had a major impact on my future life, the decisions I went on to make and the confidence she gave me to try things. She would often say that my ability at school was better than that of many other girls in my year. This was difficult for me to accept as I was reminded daily by my family of my lack of ability in anything because I could not sew, or cook properly, and never to their standard. I could do nothing good in their eyes.

At home I would lock myself in the outside toilet to avoid the physical harm that Jay in particular would cause. I became afraid to come home quite a lot, and often thought what it would be like not to have to be there. I would sometimes be in the toilet for up to two hours after school, until my father returned home. At that time I still believed that Papaji would save me from my sister's beatings. When he arrived, he would cross the yard and speak affectionately outside the toilet door, asking me to come into the house. When I crept out, he would then put his hand round my shoulder and take me in. I so wanted him to hug me, to keep me safe by his side but rarely did he ask me what had happened. I would explain between the tears and sobs. He would say little – after all, he was tired from work although he did on occasion raise the issue with my siblings and mother and tell them to leave me alone. Sometimes he would joke with them about it, so I never felt it was taken seriously, but at least I felt safe enough to come out of the toilet. My mother said nothing; she seemed totally absent and unaware of my existence. But by now I was used to that total lack of concern from her.

Early on, I was introduced to the choir alongside others in my class. I recall singing in many musicals such as *Daniel in the Lion's Den* and *Joseph and the Amazing Technicolour Dreamcoat*. There were songs like *Kumbaya my Lord, Kumbaya*, and Bob Dylan and the Beatles, and of course Cliff Richard – Pat was a huge Cliff fan. Music opened up a whole new world to me. I loved singing with others to produce beautiful harmonies. The being together was really important to me. Soon, Christian hymns became comfortingly familiar and an important part of my life. We sang Gospel music too – the 1960's Gospel influence was still around – and hymns from more recent Church influences. I sang in a choir throughout the whole time I was at school; most of the girls in the choir were from the Caribbean and I eventually formed good relationships with them, although to start with I had to fight hard for this. Britain was overcautious, if not generating racism, towards all the ethnic minority groups, blacks, Asians, and Jews. So there was a level of suspicion on the part of us all in terms of whom we could trust. Things would be said very overtly on the street to us by some white British people. I experienced bullying like many Asian girls had from some of the white girls at school. My Caribbean friends initially found it hard to accept that an Asian girl wanted to be their friend, because their own experience of Asian people had not been good due to discrimination towards them. The one thing about me was that I had faced enough rejection from within my family not to keep trying. I had kept trying with members of my family to be loved, although at home, each time the 'trying' would be punished, but I was not about to give up with my friends at school too. Soon, our bodies were swaying in unison as we belted out those moving hymns, accompanied by Pat who conducted us with enthusiastically waving arms and a big smile.

The friendships I made at school were inevitably with girls who were 'different'. I was drawn to them. Partly this was because I felt different, but partly because I felt that I leaned towards those who experienced similar things. I met a Sikh girl, Bimla, who had lived with her family in China. She was withdrawn and nervous and worked very hard to look after the house. There were other Asian girls who had difficulties at home. One thing in common amongst them was the responsibility they had to take for housework, cooking and looking after siblings; the pressure affected them greatly. I also felt from what they said about their home lives that their own needs were neglected by their families and they almost certainly experienced emotional issues like me. I knew this from the anxiety they expressed about their circumstances.

I was often told, on my return from school, to make the chapatti dough. It felt like a punishment rather than a task we might share, so I used to put it off for as long as possible. I felt that I could not be a child; I had not been spoken to as a friend of the family, so the dismissal of me in this area was often the cause of my reluctance, not just the physical punishment meted out, of which I remained fearful. On one occasion there was more chaos in the kitchen than usual as we all rushed around trying to get my father's dinner ready in time. My mother and siblings were at screaming point when he arrived home, clearly drunk. I was at the kitchen sink working over the chapatti dough in a miserable sulk – Jay had held my ear and dragged me to the kitchen by force. I recall her wet hands and anger and the shouting which was still going on. Suddenly, I heard Papaji's angry voice. There was arguing between my father, mother and my siblings. To my horror, as I turned I saw him grab hold of a knife which we used to cut vegetables which he then brought down and stabbed into my left hand between my thumb and forefinger. There was blood and shock and tears. I have blocked out exactly what happened and why Papaji even did this and remember little of events afterwards, other than Ambi dressing my wound with a bandage. With the benefit of hindsight this incident occurred because of the tensions that existed in the family and the difficulties with communication – I was often however the scapegoat for these events as the youngest female in the home. To this day, I still wear the small scar – on the inside as well as the outside. The family all treated me well for a while after that and I was told by Ambi not to say anything to anyone about what had happened. At school I became withdrawn. Pat would be there to pick me up, she asked what went on, why I was wearing the bandages; I said nothing, protecting my family. In the early seventies, child protection wasn't quite the same as it is today but I also knew that Pat did not want to make things more difficult for me at home. Many years later when I briefly shared those experiences with Pat, she said that she had always suspected the abuse that we suffered.

My teenage years passed with events that would have been familiar to many of my peers from similar backgrounds. One day my periods started and I remember being completely bewildered and scared by what was happening. I dared not approach my mother about the subject as I feared her response, too afraid of her ridicule and lack of empathy. She had never discussed such things with me, nor had my sisters. I did not know the language of puberty and periods; instead I left clues for my sister Ambi – complaints of sickness and stomach ache – until finally she provided me with sanitary wear; my mother never knew and never brought the subject up. I learnt to survive periods and hide my shame from my mother who seemed to have no idea that I might need her to explain what was happening and how to handle the pain.

One day I received a school report saying that my Maths results were very poor and that I talked too much in class. I remember feeling frustrated: I found Maths hard but, like many children in the class, never got the help needed to progress, mainly because there were too many children for the teacher to manage, and I probably did talk in class as I never found the outlet at home to do this. The teacher could not know what the consequences of this would be for me at home but I was severely chastised by my parents, especially for the shame it brought to the family. In the end, my father refused to sign and return the report, unless Jay did the homework with me. I knew Jay's methods did not involve patience and I could see that she was furious about it. I wanted Jay to love me so much, but didn't understand that perhaps she didn't know how to. She normally avoided sitting next to me and was always impatient with me. Within a few minutes of us starting to look through the exercises, she hit me very hard with her wooden Scholl sandal, right across my head, shouting at me and pulling my hair – I was terrified. The Maths lesson was over and my problems with the subject were unresolved.

When I was thirteen, things started to change. Our home life became both more domesticated and more religious. Obviously at that time I was becoming a young woman. I was aware that at this point in a girl's life, both the family and society's attitude towards her alters. She needs to be prepared for marriage and not do anything that might damage her reputation and put the prospective groom's family off. Sewing and cooking were encouraged although I was never trusted enough with anything more than mending holes and was never shown how to make a salwar kameez. I would have to stand and watch the sabji being made. If

I asked what to do, I was never shown with any enthusiasm. Although their lack of faith in my abilities affected me all my life, I am grateful that I watched, as I now cook many things drawn from my memory of how my mother chopped and sliced, grated and ground, how many pinches of this and that she added, and I am good at sewing ladders in tights! This was learnt from home and the basic knitting taught to me in primary school. We were good at looking after our clothes and preparing them the night before for wear on the following day. Hygiene and cleanliness were instilled into us, which were all good things.

Religion was more complicated. It was a part and parcel of our grooming to become good women, but learning about the Sikh way of life was very important for us because these were the things that my parents naturally valued, and I know that they took much comfort from their beliefs.

Some time before I started secondary school, Ambi had found a Sunday morning activity at a Church through a link with a teacher at school and this had been accepted by the family. In fact, it was a Sunday school and I remember her bringing home a Bible and reading me passages from it. My parents didn't oppose this, in fact, like many Sikhs they considered that it was a good thing to learn about other cultures' teachings about kindness and to think about spiritual things, although I am not sure how much of this they understood in the context of Christian beliefs and practices. At the time I was enjoying learning about Jesus at primary school and was interested, so I asked to go to the Sunday school with Ambi. She took me and I loved listening to the lessons. At the start of secondary school, I began to develop a deeper interest in Christianity when I was introduced to the more personal and direct relationship that was possible with God. Pat was a Christian and I attended prayer meetings at the school with her. These meetings were open to anyone who wanted to go. I learnt that I could pray directly to God; this was something that my parents never talked about. In Sikhism, I understood that there were set prayers for morning and night time and other special events, but as I understood it, we were not supposed to bring our concerns directly to God, instead we were supposed to find the strength to overcome these things on our own, through meditation and prayer. I realised that unlike them, I didn't believe in reincarnation, nor the belief that you would have a bad life if you did not adhere rigidly to your culture. I heard this a lot, people often talked about it when they came to visit, or when gossiping at weddings. I wanted to believe in a God who was like a father to me, who cared for me and what happened to me, and that my fate did not have to be decided by the rules of a culture which I did not accept. My mother would say bitterly, "Your life will be a bad one, your karma is not good." I had respect for my parents' beliefs because there were many good things about Sikhism and its practices, but to be able to talk directly to God whenever I wanted was a huge release, especially with what was happening at home. I could actually tell God about the problems in the family and ask that they would all be safe. The lack of expression and emotion at home was focused in my prayers to God. This was a turning point for me. I felt that God was with me and that He would not let any harm come to me; from then on, everything revolved around this and I escaped into a world where things were safe. I finally had something for myself, something special and meaningful. My teacher Pat never said that I should ignore the Sikh teachings, in fact she showed me pictures of the Gurus and explained that they were good people who taught righteous living, bringing Muslims, Hindus, Christians and Sikhs together in truth, despite the disharmony we saw around us and lived within.

Pat organised prayer meetings after school for those who were interested and I was keen to attend (as were many others). I asked my mother if I could stay behind for this – I would need to be at school until 5pm, sometimes 5.30pm. I remember working myself up to asking her, terrified that she would refuse. Initially she saw nothing wrong with me doing so. Again, her reaction did not totally surprise me: from her point of view, I was out of the way and so long as I returned home before my father, the discussion about where I had been would not be raised. In fact, my parents were aware of the fact that I was reading my Bible even though I tried not to make it obvious. And whilst they had chosen to send me to an English school, as time went by they were becoming increasingly conscious that we were straying from our traditional

Sikh ways. Perhaps they were seeing the aspects of Ambi's behaviour that we were both so desperate to hide. When she was twelve, they told Ambi that she couldn't go to Sunday school any longer because she was getting too old to be out without a chaperone.

Not long after this, they sent me to Punjabi school for religious lessons instead; there I was supposed to learn to read Sikh scriptures and behave like a proper Sikh. I went with my two paternal cousins who by then had moved with their families to the same area as us. Every Saturday we were trusted to go on a bus, quite a long way, and I enjoyed going because it got me out of the house. On one occasion my cousins, who lived on the same road as me, were unable to go, so I had to make the trip alone. On the way home, I was very nearly run over. I must have been about eleven years old at the time and I was not used to travelling this kind of distance on my own. I was very nervous and the road I had to cross once I'd got off the bus was very busy. I had to take a chance when I could. I'd stood there an awfully long time, the problem being that there were cars parked so I couldn't really see what was coming. I peered out again and it looked safe so I ran out but someone had pulled out of a side street and was coming straight towards me! I skidded, the car screeched to a halt and I fell in front of it, feeling the heat of the wheels and the road. I lay there for a moment or two but before the driver could get out, I stood up and shakily walked away. The car drove off and I stumbled home, my heart hammering in my chest. Although I wasn't badly injured, the experience really shook me up and I was still sobbing when I arrived home. My mother was in the kitchen and when I saw her, the words came tumbling out. I told her what had happened, desperate to fall into her arms and be hugged and comforted. Instead she lifted her glasses, looked at me coldly and walked off saying over her shoulder, "You should be more careful."

I continued to go to the Punjabi school on the bus and learnt to recite the morning prayer and parts of the evening prayer and the teacher said that I was clever. My parents also expected me to attend services at the Gurdwara regularly. We would go as a family, sometimes on weekday evenings as well as weekends. I would go, sit for what seemed like hours and meditate when I could. This was a very confusing time as my mainstream English schooling had given me faith in Jesus and it was difficult to know what to believe. As time went by the pressure for me to learn about and conform to the Sikh religion increased and, as well as going to the Gurdwara and Punjabi school, I was expected to sit with the family in the lounge for the evening prayer. I had no understanding of what was being read or what it meant as it was never explained to me. I tried hard to make sense of it but was confused between the things I had learnt about God at school and my family's religion. What I was told about their beliefs seemed illogical to me as they expressed it almost exclusively in terms of women covering up and being subservient and having to bow down before the Gurus. Yet my lessons had also taught me that Gurus were good teachers who did good deeds, just like Jesus who was my teacher at this time.

One day I returned home with a banjo that someone had given me at my English school. I sat down to play some of the music we played on the guitars at school, which I loved and which I thought my parents would not mind. I had only just started to sing when Papaji jumped to his feet, pulled the banjo out of my hands and smashed it against the wall. He shouted that I should be growing up and not doing music; he forbade me from doing these activities at school and said that I could have nothing more to do with my Christian teacher. I told him I wouldn't, but I couldn't imagine my days at school without the loving concern I got from Pat. I was simply more careful what I brought home. These things created for me two separate worlds, and the secrets of one could not be shared in the other.

Around this time, although a bit idealistic, I felt I wanted to change the things I saw going on around me and had already thought about doing social work, not understanding at this time how stable you have to be to manage this. Looking back I was trying to mend the situation around me, of my life at home. One day when talking to Pat about 'East versus West' issues (as we would call them), she suggested that I should start a discussion group for the Asian girls at our school. I think she could see how torn we were between the lives we led at home and what we were learning at school, caught between the two cultures. All I wanted was to be able to see my teachers and friends outside school, go on outings with them, play with them in the park, or meet together at one of the houses where they had events arranged by the Church groups. They were simple and innocent enough things, but I would hardly ever be allowed to go. I attended my teacher's wedding and went on two outings – a visit to a school in London which Pat had organised for the Asian girls, and a picnic in the park organised by the Church.

I think she also suggested the group so that we could share some of the things we were clearly not happy about. I was just twelve years of age. All the girls who joined were facing the same kind of problems at home as me, and like me, had no one they could unburden themselves upon. To talk about such things with strangers was considered extremely shameful, yet we could not talk about them with our families either. Many of them worked very hard at looking after younger siblings and cooking and cleaning and sewing, they were often very tired when they came to school, and school was like an escape, like a privilege not to be missed... that's how we felt about school. It was never boring, this was where we met and talked to people we would not be allowed to speak with in our neighbourhoods, friends we could not invite around because they were white.

It was arranged that we would meet in one of the classrooms during lunch hour and I would chair the meeting. This ended up being an exhausting task as the girls would talk on top of one another and I had to try to get them to speak one at a time! The group was kept secret from our families but it was clear that these girls needed to talk, and I identified with their pain. The group – there were usually between six and ten of us – carried on for several years. We did talk about marriage and other serious issues that we would sometimes end up laughing about, perhaps because it was such a relief to share the pain. At home, we could never express our feelings and emotions, we just had to accept that this is how things were, but here we were questioning if this was right or not. It was interesting how many of the girls thought that marriage might be an escape from the workload at home. They argued how much better it would be to be able to do what you wanted in your own home without someone nagging you to do other things; this was more appealing and possibly an escape from the cultures and traditions that we felt were oppressive. Then we would talk about mothers-in-law, and hope that we would not have to face being subservient to one. We might not have understood everything, but we certainly freely expressed our concerns and fears, and that brought us together. I had five close friends as a result who remained so throughout my school years. As Sikh girls, we could never meet outside of the school gates, which seemed strange to me, as if the world between school and community had to be separated, but our adventures whilst we were in school were very important and significant in our development. We laughed a great deal, but we knew that most of us would have marriages arranged when we left school. Our greatest hope was that some of us would go to college or university; that would be a big step as most of the girls' parents expected them to get jobs to help save for their dowries. I know now that my friends were all married soon after they left school and none of them went to college. I heard that one or two worked in the factories until they had saved enough to pay for the privilege of not being mistreated, which is what dowries really represent. The practice was banned in India in 1961 but is still commonplace. It is believed that up to 25,000 Indian women are killed every year in India because of the inability or refusal of their families to make sufficient payments to the family of the groom. It is also the reason why many female babies are killed at birth. Dowries also continue to show the prestige and wealth of the family before a daughter is handed over to the other family.

All these discussions began to confirm my worst fears: that school was not only a temporary period for me but less important than preparation for my arranged marriage. Although I loved school, I did experience some bullying, due to my size and colour. Even so, I had made enough friends there to keep me going for a lifetime. I was also made deputy head girl, which was a surprise to me: I think I got this because the teachers were on my side and wanted me to do well. Standing up for myself despite my size was a great boost to my confidence. The subject of my marriage had been spoken of often since I was eleven years old, as this was a way of preparing girls and instilling in them the need to behave honourably. Neighbours and relatives would comment on how many girls my parents had, and how expensive it would be for them to provide dowries and organise our marriages... as if to add to their shame.

I overheard my mother having conversations with relatives who visited and also the neighbour who already looked out for the honour of my family especially when we arrived home in our too-short school skirts (even though they were below the knee!). The conversation between my mother and neighbour would go:

"Penji, what can we do? Where will we find a match for a girl of her colour and size?" and "Girls have to learn to sew and cook and she is not interested!"

I was surprised at my mother saying this as she had never shown me how to sew. I could not say anything because it was disrespectful for a young woman to give her point of view to an older person. I had been taught early enough to "Keep quiet or else".

Secrets therefore seemed to me to serve no other purpose than to divide the world around me, to maintain conformity to honour at any cost to individuals; it left confusion in my growing years, so that I did not know whom to trust. I felt that if we were able to share the world of school at home with our parents then there would be no reason to keep such secrets, and children could grow up knowing that they could trust their parents and confide in them; and that it was not wrong to learn through talking about things openly. I often wondered what the potential for change could have been for my family if we had been able to talk with each other, rather than worry what impact sharing information might have on us all.

Chapter 4

Teenage Years

"An honor code or honor system is a set of rules or principles governing a community based on a set of rules or ideals that define what constitutes honorable behavior within that community. The use of an honor code depends on the idea that people (at least within the community) can be trusted to act honorably. Those who are in violation of the honor code can be subject to various sanctions, including expulsion from the institution."

(Wikipedia)

The constant tinkling and clanging of cymbals and harmonium can be heard up and down the street. Despite ours being small terraced house, in the small space of our front room are some ten or twelve Sikh women as well as many of our immediate relatives and neighbours. My mother is having a gathering called a 'Sathsang'; this is a music based praise, devotion and meditation session, commonplace during the seventies in our families. The Sikh women present are all wearing white chunnis on their heads, their eyes are lowered in prayer, they are deep in song and meditation; sweat is pouring from their faces. My mother has organised this with my aunt, who has become a promising leader of such events for Sikh women.

I am almost fourteen years old and am being primed for my role as a subservient Sikh woman, however I am just as aware that traditions play a part in the moulding of women: I must cover my head, dress modestly, sit cross-legged and listen to words that I don't understand. They are in Gurmukhi, which sounds beautiful, even if I don't understand the full meaning. I try to appreciate my mother's role in this and yet I cannot feel the religious transformation that is supposed to be happening inside me. The women can only say that it is good to listen to the 'Bani', they do not explain what it means. I struggle to comprehend, I have a mind that questions in hope of understanding, not a mind that fits in with what others say is right. *Why do I have to be different?* This is a question that I have struggled with for as long as I can remember. Ambi is impatient with me:

"It's just the way things are and you have to accept it," she says. She is angry and the furrows on her brow make me feel guilty for asking what these things mean.

"Why do you have to be different?" she echoes. With this, she picks herself up and storms off to the next room. Over the years, I have begun to realise that Ambi is not cross with me; she is cross with the world, with her lot, with her secret. I seem to remind her of what it is like to have the freedom to think for yourself; she doesn't need to be reminded of that loss too.

When I started at the secondary modern school, I regularly went in with egg-shaped lumps on my head, which I got from being hit with the Scholl. The lumps were sore and they hurt, and whilst I came to accept them as normal after a time, my emotions and the bruises to my self-respect were harder to manage. I spent a great deal of time on my own when home. I would dread the summer holidays. I remember reading books like *What Katie Did*, about families a world away from my experiences. When I was younger I would spend hours with lollipop sticks, poking at the dirt between the slabs; sometimes I would play hopscotch, or make-believe. I wanted to be like the girls at school, the English kids who always made up wonderful fantasies when they played together. I really was in a world of my own, reciting nursery rhymes and singing to myself; it was an escape from the reality of life. As I got older, those games obviously lost their appeal although I would still fantasise about the future I could have, as at home I was very lonely.

When younger it was rare to have children come to play with me but occasionally Bimla, the Sikh girl I met in primary school and who lived across the road, would be allowed. She was a very cautious and worried-looking child, always watching the clock so she would not get in trouble for being late home. Some time before, I had heard whispers between my mother and father, and then later between my mother and a neighbour who often visited, that Bimla's seventeen year old sister had run away – she had escaped during the night from an upstairs window. She was a beautiful girl as I recall, and the family were always very protective of her. I soon learnt that she had run off with a Muslim boy, which I knew was forbidden for a Sikh girl. For some years afterwards this incident played on my mind. The family disowned her – why would they do that? Why was what she did so terrible? From inside the Sikh community we never heard if attempts were made by the girl to reconcile, we were simply told that she had dishonoured the family and community. The parents behaved as if she had died, especially the mother who lost weight and withdrew. Even Bimla became more and more distant from me; she was instructed by her parents to be on her best behaviour all the time and not to get involved in anything outside of the home. She was not allowed to talk about it. I knew that as soon as she finished school she would have an arranged marriage to save the honour of the family. This was my first experience of hearing about a girl who had dishonoured her family because of her choice to go with a boy she loved. I thought about it a lot. Would Bimla's sister miss her family? I wondered if perhaps she would be better off without them, since she was as restricted at home as we were. I envied her freedom and admired her bravery for making that choice.

The times I was happiest were when Ambi and I went upstairs to our shared bedroom, laid down on our beds and secretly listened to the pop charts on the radio. This was usually on a Sunday, when our favourite songs were played. In between the records we would talk, speculating about what had happened to Bimla's sister and exchanging what information we knew about other girls at school whose lives were so difficult because of family expectations. Ambi had left school by then and had a job in a local hospital. She needed to earn money for her dowry and to buy things she wanted for herself. Sometimes she would tell me about her relationship with the boy she was still seeing. The conversations always started with her saying, "You won't tell, will you? But such and such has happened…" Then she would look worried, until I reassured her that I would never say a word. Sometimes we discussed what was happening in our family. There were difficulties that my parents had to regularly sort out between themselves and relatives about marriages in our family. The pressure on Jay to conform was mounting – she had been promised to a family, however the parameters between compatibility and tradition were blurred. Jay did not have the opportunity that I believe she needed to get to know her future husband.

I recall little about the events leading up to the wedding. I think I shut it out of my mind for some reason. Perhaps I realised I would soon be free from her abuse, that she would no longer be able to make me feel like I did not matter. I was the one on whom she would take out her frustrations and anger, and soon I would no longer be there for her to do this. I don't know why she never accepted me, and I feared her. I remember the hard slaps, the shouting and banging doors, her being upset with everyone in the house; I wonder now if she was depressed. This would not surprise me, as our mother was not able to relate emotionally to any of us and her poor health affected us all; it felt as though Jay was angry with her for being like this. What I do remember is that the wedding was kept very quiet, as Jay was considered to be too outspoken and educated, and subservience was considered far more important.

Of course, I understood that the men we were to marry would be chosen for us by both the immediate and the extended family, carefully selected from within the clan. The men's mindset would be the same traditional one we had been brought up with and the expectation of us as women would be to conform to our community's rules. We had no option but to obey, whether we wanted to or not. Still, it didn't stop several girls – including Ambi, of course – from having boyfriends before they got married, even though the relationship could not last. If the two fell in love, their only option was to disappear, like Bimla's sister had done. Some girls were also made to 'disappear' by their families – I had heard of such things happening but found these so called "honour" crimes. I had also heard of women being killed, I did not know the term 'honour killing' then, but I did know that women's lives could be made very difficult if they did not submit and obey; that divorce was frowned upon, and that many men and women suffered in silence in marriages that they did not want to be in but accepted as something that they had to make the most of. However I heard stories from my parents about girls who had been killed in the Punjab. I may not have called them honour killings then, but I knew deep down that these women were never at fault; the problem was that they had spoken out, or just displeased someone.

"It was their karma," my mother would say. "There was nothing they could have done about what happened to them."

I knew that there were very few choices for women. Many girls left school at sixteen and flew back to India or Pakistan to get married. Noor was married by the age of seventeen. Ambi would remind me that our lives were not that bad: we were allowed to go to work (albeit because they knew we would be saving for our dowries) and that this was liberated compared to some parents; we were able to wear the clothes we wanted, up to a point (flared trousers rather than salwar kameez; skirts at school, even though we had to hide our knees when we came home). She also pointed out the sacrifices our parents made in order to bring us to Britain, the years of hard work in Africa and the poverty in India. She reminded me about their bad health and said that we should be grateful to them for bringing us into the world and caring for us, and that we must repay them by caring for them. I had no disagreement with that, despite the poor relationship between Mamaji and me. I was just frightened about the prospect of a marriage with a stranger and having no part in the decision-making process. I began to take more notice of the stories that I occasionally overheard.

A distant relative's daughter died, and the rumour was that she had committed suicide as a result of the domestic violence she suffered. The adults were very good at keeping things like this quiet, and talking in the community was frowned upon. You would be blamed for talking and making judgement. I also remember stories about a cousin who had problems in her marriage which affected my family so badly that they fell out about it. It was extremely difficult for women to come out of marriages that did not work. Everything would be done to keep the couple together and help from the extended family was considered essential to right such problems, when what was clearly needed was independent support for the victim. However, for my father and generations before him, going outside of the family was seen as a weakness, a lack of loyalty, and almost certainly a betrayal of the trust of the family.

At fifteen, my interest in boys was more curiosity than any wish to get involved in something. In many respects, I was innocent. The Indian girls at school had secret boyfriends and Ambi continued to see hers, so this curiosity did not seem particularly wrong for me, as long as my parents didn't find out; the importance of secrecy was after all what I had been taught by them, both in actions and words. The boys at school had just moved to our all-girls' school, so we were now co-ed. For a while, a boy called Balbir followed me around the cloakrooms with a big grin. He wore a turban, which I thought looked very smart on him. He had a happy view of life, and was loved by his family. We quickly made friends and surprisingly, this is how we stayed for a long time; he was someone I could talk to. We walked home together, and since my family had recently moved to another part of the city, there was enough distance in-between my home and the school in Handsworth for it to be unlikely that we would be seen. However, we wanted more time together, so instead of going straight home we'd walk out of school in the opposite direction and venture to paths further afield, strolling hand in hand, kissing from time to time, but mainly talking. It felt wonderful to be out in the fresh air, like a holiday. This had been my first experience of doing something away from my own family without control and restriction, and although I knew that what I was doing was wrong, it was also great to feel so free, to feel good about myself, to know that someone liked me. I didn't talk to Ambi much about this and when I did, all she said was, "Don't let anyone find out."

As the months went by, although we did not spend a lot of time together, we probably became a little too relaxed about things and one day we were seen by Balbir's brother from the top of his road, not far from school. In this culture, the siblings – especially the brothers – are the keepers and the parents have to be prevented from knowing at all costs. It can often be the children who take responsibility for the family's honour.

The next day I didn't see him at our normal meeting place. Then we broke up for the holidays, and although for several days I went back to look for him, he never showed up. I didn't really have to ask why he wasn't there: we both knew that it was not acceptable for us to be seen together because we would both have arranged marriages, and boys and girls did not see each other before that. Afterwards, once the holidays were over and we were back at school, we avoided each other and never talked about it. For a long time, I felt very sad and rejected and wondered what had been said to Balbir. I missed this happy-go-lucky person with the huge smile who laughed with me about things. But I knew that having a relationship with an Asian guy outside of the family clan was never going to be an option.

I ended up talking to Ambi about these things and it was a real comfort to me; although our special time together was short-lived, I grew to love her, following her like a shadow, copying her fashion style and the way she did her hair. When she plucked her eyebrows I did mine, and when I occasionally borrowed one of her items of clothing, she let me keep it. We loved Punjabi humour and often keeled over laughing about the different personalities we came across in Sikh families. These are the things we shared.

When I look back on these times, I think she always knew that I would leave. She must have known something about my Christian faith and how hard it would be for me to accept a Sikh husband. Also, she could not imagine that my parents would be able to find me a suitable marriage partner simply because I was so short and dark-skinned. I am sure she thought I would be a spinster living with my parents into their old age. This was not acceptable and such women were stigmatised in Asian families because they were seen as a burden to the family. Unless they were married, their worth was very little.

To our great shock and dismay, shortly after Jay got married and left home, Papaji had a heart attack; he was only in his early fifties. Despite this, he continued to work at the steel foundry. The whole family was worried about his health, and the remaining children at home – now just Ambi, me and Dev – were told by relatives and everyone who knew us that it was our responsibility not to cause undue worry to our Papaji. One look from Ambi or my older sisters when they visited told me that I should feel shame about any choices I wanted to make for myself; I should only be thinking of him. We were constantly on edge – entirely responsible, we were told, for our parents' well-being. The first heart attack was blamed on my older siblings' marriages and their husbands' apparent disrespect of my father. Of course, we could never say this to anyone else; the secrets had to be kept buried. Outside the walls of our house and the bosom of the nuclear family, we had to present everything as if it was normal. We were the best dressed family at weddings, where the women would be turned out in beautiful chunnis and the men in their starched burgundy and black turbans and the latest gentlemen's suits. The proud men with their hands in their pockets and legs apart, showing their dominance in the Ramgharia clan. The restrictions at home at this time became even more pronounced. In my primary school years I was allowed to play outside on my own and on many occasions spent hours swinging in a park some distance from the house, knowing adults were unaware and probably not too bothered where I was; but now every move had to be explained. I only had the excuse of needing to get something from the corner shop as a possible way to leave the house. It was very stifling at home, and although we watched the TV sometimes (if suitable programmes were on), the women in the family did not have much else to do other than cleaning, cooking and sewing. I began to resent it but even to this day, cleaning and cooking are instilled into me.

Chapter 5

Hopes, Dreams and Reality

"... when a man is denied the right to live the life he believes in, he has no choice but to become an outlaw."

(Nelson Mandela)

I left school with some decent GCSEs and a trial A-Level in Religious Studies. Leaving Pat was a huge personal loss to me, something that would go on to affect me into my adult years. She had, however, given me something no one else had – the ability to see within myself a potential to become anything that I wanted. She had encouraged in me an independent spirit quite opposed to the closed upbringing of the clan that I had been raised in. I saw no wrong in this, because after all is this not what we all need – to learn to thrive and reach that potential?

I applied to go to Sixth Form College to do my A-Levels. The whole thing was done by me without much reference to my parents as I feared that if given the choice they would tell me I should stay at home. When I made a passing comment about it, Papaji looked concerned. I needed his signature to process the application, due to my age.

"You're going to college?" he asked with some agitation. I explained where and what I was intending to study and that was that. He looked down, said very little, approval was not what he gave, a signature he did, and that is all I needed. I felt like a criminal asking for it. I knew that he would much rather have me stay at home and do the housework, what else could he possibly want for me?

He couldn't stop me, as Ambi had done the same and was now working. I got myself a Saturday job at Tesco as I always worried about asking my mother for money. She wouldn't make me feel very good about asking for bus fares or the like. Ambi would help me where she could. I knew that moving to a newly built house (three up one down) and paying for the dowries and marriages of four daughters had put a strain on the family finances. Our diet was very basic – mostly vegetarian – and we still lived in one of the poorest parts of Smethwick. Was I so wrong not to want more than the poverty many experienced in neighbourhoods around me? I knew the way to achieve this was through education, despite education being seen by my parents as not for women: a woman's role was to be subservient and support the structures of religious and family life.

In the autumn of 1975, I started Sixth Form College. I remember those years as a time of great personal conflict. I certainly had more freedom as the timetable at college was not as restrictive as the one at school; I did not have to attend all the lessons and we had some free periods which I spent with others in the common room and the games room / pool area. Circumstances at home made it easier for me to keep secrets from my family, since I had less and less interaction with them and no one took much interest in my education, and by now had little trust in what the future could hold for me. On the other hand, Mamaji was quite dependent on us children, having recently suffered a stroke then being diagnosed with a debilitating illness. This had devastated us all, and required major adjustment by all the family. My mother still had teenagers at home and my father at work, and although we were all fairly independent of her, she was no longer able to make the sabji or put clothes in the wash. These were not so much major changes for us as children, but for my father in particular in terms of his time focused at home on Mamaji's illness. This meant that my mother and father no longer did the visits to relatives and friends as they used to; this would all take time to do again. As soon as we came home we would have to go upstairs to give Mamaji food and tablets and see to her care. Food would be left for her upstairs for the daytime. Arrangements were not made for someone to care for her during the day – I felt sorry for her and felt very guilty that I was at college. Ambi took this role very seriously as the next in line from the siblings. My mother had become like a child herself, dependent and very emotional as this was a part of her condition. Despite having suffered a second heart attack, my father was still working hard, and of course he worried about Mamaji. We were all worried about Mamaji, and my father's retirement was some years away. Going to college, therefore, felt like I was doing the wrong thing. I also knew that soon, it would be Ambi's turn to marry and the pressure would then be on me to take on the role of being the main carer for my mother: Dev, the only boy, was not expected to carry out any duties, household or otherwise. I prayed that Ambi's marriage wouldn't happen any time soon.

Then the unthinkable happened: Ambi was caught seeing her boyfriend by a relative, somehow, somewhere. I still remember the man who informed my father, and will never forget him. I wondered what reason he would have to do this. I realised that being an informer meant that he had acted according to the set of rules in our communities, to save my father's honour. He would, of course, have to do something about it. I was not told anything about it by my parents, who still kept events like these hidden from me, as if they might somehow contaminate or influence me: it was Ambi who told me about it, tearfully. A few days later she told me that she would be getting married within the clan, which was not a surprise (in fact, I found out that she had already been promised to another family by my father sometime in the past). Now arrangements were hurriedly made for the wedding, before the scandal could leak out and ruin her reputation. In some ways, I felt that she would be relieved to leave home and all her bad memories. Still, I was devastated to be losing my sister, and soon I would be the only girl left. I had no idea what my parents had planned for me – whether I was to be married off or kept at home to care for them in their old age. At least Ambi's match looked promising: according to her, her fiancé was an educated man, so perhaps she would be treated better than Noor and Jay were by their husbands. I hoped so.

Around this time there was an incident of domestic violence in one of the close members of our extended family. Relatives as well as Papaji spent a lot of time pacing up and down, my father stroking his beard and muttering to himself while Mamaji looked on anxiously. They took a lot of responsibility for the wider extended family. After I had gone to bed, I would hear raised voices downstairs. The two families of the couple concerned had come together to resolve difficulties in the marriage. Ambi quickly ushered me upstairs and shut me in my room. I heard loud noises and raised voices, what sounded like threats and then a scuffle and shouts. I was terrified that someone had been hurt and didn't know what to do and remember climbing into bed and pulling the blankets over my head; shortly afterwards a police car arrived. Later on, Ambi explained the little that she understood (since it was not discussed in front of us by my parents), but I was never sure how much she really knew. I grew up knowing that marriages had their problems but these were secret affairs which had to be kept hidden behind closed doors. Superstition also prevailed in this society, and it was as though the less you spoke of bad things, somehow the less likely they were to happen.

Public shame and knowledge of arranged marriages going wrong were too hard for our families to accept, as the responsibilities for these were often shared by families, not only the couple. I remember that disgraced women would often visit their parents without their husbands or families knowledge. The traditions of my family's culture dictated that once a girl was married, she was the property of her husband, and for her to publicly reject the match the families had made was seen as a great insult. Women would find it hard to accept this; as well as being told that they could not pursue a career in their own right, the reality about what they could do to save the marriage was often also restricted within the realms of what they were allowed to do, i.e. seeking counselling or help in a refuge was contrary to family values of keeping it within the family. Whilst my father obviously did what he could to support difficulties in marriages, his hands were often tied since the man's side of the family had more ownership to the marriage than the woman's side.

In later years I also learnt of many women in the families that we knew suffering from depression. I had concerns for my sisters' marriages; I felt for them and had cried for them, despite their hardness towards me. They did not deserve the life that was chosen for them by my parents, and it broke my heart to see their strong, free spirits being crushed by subservience.

During my teenage years I withdrew more and more into myself. There were long periods of silence in my life. It was during this time that I started thinking of a better future than my parents could give or provide. Noor and Jay were married, Ambi would be soon and I could see from their journeys that mine would not be any easier. Was it so selfish to want to have a life without the oppression that existed for women I had known? Could I be so blind as to think that everything would be alright marrying into tradition and subservience? I knew that some young women at school, and later college, would hope and trust that their parents made the right choice, but what a gamble.

In my two years at Sixth Form, I became increasingly confused and distant, dreading the future that lay ahead. There was no question about it – marriage was the only way that I would be able to leave home. I was not sure that my life would be any different to my sisters'. I'm sure that I only managed to survive this period because of the contact that I had in college with my friends; I was in the 'Asian group' and the 'Christian Union' group. The Asian group rebelled against everything; they organised outings to parks far away from the sight of nosey family and neighbours, snogged in the common rooms, did anything but real work at college. Some of them smoked cigarettes and defied their parents. I would hop between this and the Christian Union group, although I sought my identity within both. I was curious as to how my girlfriends in the Asian group were going to manage having serious relationships with boys at college knowing that they were going to be faced with an arranged marriage. My friends Anthea and Baldeep, who were Christians, held me together through this period, more than any identity to either of these groups. Baldeep and I were clear that we did not want arranged marriages, and did not want a life of restriction and what this could potentially mean for us. I knew that she meant this, although looking back, at seventeen, we were idealistic. These relationships, however, shaped what would to some extent give us courage for what would later happen.

ELO was playing in the common room: the track was *Sweet Talking Woman.* The Asian kids were discovering their identity in both worlds.

"Hey yar!" someone called out. I recognised this phrase – a mixture of English and Punjabi ('Yar' meaning brother or friend). This sounded like a voice of reason to me.

It was Kam, a Ramgharia Sikh boy sporting a burgundy Kenyan-style turban and huge flared 70s jeans. Kenyan-styled turbans had either small peaks to the top of the turban or no peak at all. One look and I was smitten. He hung around with the Asian group and had been primed by the others to chat me up, to see if he could get a date with me. He was almost six foot tall and I was well below his armpit! I wasn't bothered; there was something I liked about this boy and we began to spend lot of time together. Kam was a refreshing friendship that I needed at this very depressing time at home, someone to talk to, who might love me for who I was. Kam and I remained friends for the two years of Sixth Form. The relationship did not go further than hugging and kissing, but his friendship was incredibly important to me throughout the lonely years at home. He would listen sympathetically to my problems and we talked about how very different it was being brought up in our culture as a boy rather than a girl. His brothers however, were fierce – his keepers, like my sisters had been mine. Kam, like Balbir at school, was fearful of being found out by them and we both felt very trapped in this secret relationship. We did not discuss what would happen into the future; he did not know how his family would respond to us being together, and I suppose I realised that it would be a very 'Big Ask' if he ever had to tell them. We were living in a time when relationships outside of marriage were forbidden. They would make big news in the community, despite us knowing that many of our friends in the college also had these forbidden relationships. That was the irony of it all. My attitude to this was different – by now, I had made up my mind. I was having none of it, not after seeing the matches for my siblings and the miserable lives they lived. I approached life with a newfound courage, determined that I would not conform and give in to a life of unhappiness, being treated without a shred of respect and expected to keep quiet no matter what anyone did to me. I would not let them force me to marry someone I didn't know – I wanted to make my own choices. Even though deep down we both knew nothing more could come of it, Kam and I continued to see each other because of our special friendship. And then, the unthinkable happened.

Papaji came home from work one evening and sat on the sofa after his meal, opening the post. He pulled what looked like photographs out of a brown envelope and froze. He wouldn't look me in the eye but I knew that this had something to do with me. He stood up suddenly.

"Tell that boy I want to see him," he shouted, rattling the photographs in front of my face as he walked out of the room.

I just had time to see that they were of Kam and me sitting on a park bench. They were never handed to me, and to this day I have no idea what my father did with these photos. I vaguely remembered a man with a camera walking past us once and looking but it never occurred to me that someone was actually following us to get evidence, which is what it turned out they had done. I suspected Kam's brothers – they must have hired someone to do it. My heart sank. The atmosphere was awful as Papaji walked away. My mother sat there wide-eyed and then launched into me, saying that I had no shame and she didn't know what my father would do and other very hurtful things. She knew my prospects for marriage would be even more limited if this got out. I went and hid in my room. When I next saw Kam, I told him what had happened and he said that he would talk to my father. I felt a mixture of shame and guilt at conducting a relationship with Kam and the family not knowing about this for almost two years.

One Saturday morning, the doorbell rang. My father opened the door and there, to my horror, was Kam. My hand flew to my mouth: I never imagined that he would come to the house. What would Papaji say, or do, to him? I suspected Kam had come in order to avoid my father confronting his brothers and the rest of his family about the relationship which would then make it public and personal, a matter of honour. Kam never said this but I knew. He was no more ready than I was to be open about us having a relationship and in any case he knew we would never be allowed to go any further. His family would not agree to him marrying me, even though we were from the same clan.

Papaji hustled Kam away from the front door and into the garage where they wouldn't be seen by prying eyes. They weren't there that long, but by the time I heard Kam leave I was feeling that my whole world had caved in, and seeing Kam meant everything to me at this time. There was no one else in my life I could really open up to and trust other than him. It was so difficult in the seventies to communicate with people outside of your home, as the phone was not so readily available and going out of the house was not possible without good reason or permission. I would have to wait now to hear from Kam. After a while I crept downstairs. Papaji did not look at me. He just said, "That's it, Kam is best forgotten now." I dreaded what else would now happen.

I never got to find out what was said between them. I imagine that my father asked him if he was just messing around or if he intended to marry me (perhaps he thought it was a good idea – he knew how hard it would be to find a husband for me in the UK as matches were hard to find for the number of women to men) and that Kam told him about his brothers and that it would not be allowed. I believe my father may have gone to talk to Kam's family about it, but the only result was that to my great sadness, Kam disappeared from my life. Although I would have had little contact with him as we had just finished college, he used to come looking for me, but all that stopped. He had clearly been told not to have any contact with me and I can only guess that he had been threatened, or given an ultimatum. I was devastated. Kam was the person I talked to about what was happening at home, he was aware of all the things that were going on, he would listen and understand. This was all gone. I was grieving I think, and this loss of friendship and comfort affected me badly. I became even more depressed, and there was no one to talk to about this whole thing. I knew he had been serious about me and I felt very let down when he did not stand up for our relationship. I thought he should have had the courage to say that he would continue to see me and make something of this relationship. I did not understand that Kam had stronger ties with his family than I did – in my family, no one appeared to care what happened to me, but he was very loyal to his brothers. I also thought that our relationship was quite a strong one; we had been together for two years, so why was he not prepared to fight for us as I would have done? Would it always be like this with Asian boys? I would see around me that they would have white girlfriends but they never fought for these relationships and eventually ended up in marriages arranged by their parents to someone from the same clan. The cost of not conforming was high. Why did it have to be like this? It took me years to get over the loss of Kam. He had to return to his clan, otherwise he would be punished. It was over a year before I saw him again, when he casually called to see me at the place where I was working. I hid my broken heart and we had a quick chat but it was difficult to keep my emotions hidden. Kam was my first real love.

The fallout from my being seen with Kam was immediate. There were 'secret' conversations and I was avoided, the family obviously busy making arrangements but not saying anything to me. It was all horribly familiar; they were looking for a match for me. During those months for various reasons there were constant arguments between members of the family and also increasing pressure on me to conform to being a 'good Sikh girl'. They knew I held Christian beliefs even though I never pushed this in their faces, but now there was increasing concern about my reading the Bible. I felt very guilty about this because I knew that it would not be acceptable for me to go outside the religion I was raised in. The pressure increased on me to attend Sikh services and spend time in Sikh prayers in the evenings without any reason given for why this was expected. I conformed through pressure, but still saw my Christian beliefs as the right way for me; I had no particular issue with the principles of Sikhism, rather I had found another way to channel my spiritual life. My relationship with my teachers was also seen as a bad influence which was not compatible with their plans for an arranged marriage.

Looking back I can see that my father was only doing what he felt was right, but all this eventually led to me taking an overdose. Ambi found me in bed and must have guessed something was up; she lifted the duvet and asked me what was wrong, what had I done? There wasn't a lot to say, and before I knew it, I was at the hospital and my stomach was being pumped to remove the paracetamol I'd taken. I had lost all will to live; I felt that there was no one who would understand or who I could talk to. It was never a serious attempt, but a cry for help.

At the hospital I was asked if I wanted to see a social worker and I agreed, thinking that I might be helped to find a way out of the situation at home. I had a few sessions with an elderly lady who I got on quite well with; we discussed various things including the possibility of a respite or convalescence period, but one day she suddenly said our meetings were over, the reason being that "my family may not like it". I felt cheated; it seemed as though my family's feelings were more of a worry to her than my well-being and health. I thought I might have been offered the chance of leaving home and starting a new life; it would have been the perfect way to escape an already hostile situation and the inevitable threat of a marriage partner not of my choice. I was too exhausted and tearful to understand where she was coming from.

When I returned home, Ambi was the only one who would speak to me. She was kinder than she was towards me previously. The family had been told by the hospital not to put me under any pressure because I was unhappy. Ambi knew this but she didn't know what to do and continued to point out that I needed to conform. The silence and lack of support and communication again confused and upset me. No mention was ever made by my parents of these events; it was as if they never happened. The silence as always was deafening, a denial of my existence or needs. On my return to school, the college counsellor saw me. He was an extrovert man, short and tubby with greying hair and a great sense of humour, and he was worried about me, would talk with me and listen. Eventually he called a meeting at my home. By all rules and standards in the family, this would be seen as intrusive, yet somehow he had arranged it – my parents and several other people were there, including our GP (who was Asian) and one of the college tutors. I felt incredibly uncomfortable – this was never going to be a good idea. The counsellor had not grasped the issue of shame; he had misjudged the effects of having this meeting in the house. My parents felt they had no choice but to go ahead with it, despite the fact that they found it very difficult; they were from a generation of people who believed that anything to do with government agencies (and that included school) was unquestionable but it was clear they were embarrassed. Unsurprisingly, very little was said at the time, but afterwards my parents told me how shameful this was for them and I had to suffer Ambi's usual chastisement that I would never learn; but it wasn't me who had wanted this meeting.

I went to collect my A-Level results at the end of the summer. I had wanted to do social work from as young an age as I could remember, and was excited to have been offered a conditional place at Moray House in Scotland. When I opened the envelope, my heart sank. My grades were – perhaps unsurprisingly – not good enough to get into university. I was bitterly disappointed, not just because it seemed as though I would not be able to follow the career I had dreamed of, but also because this was to be my escape, although as yet unknown to my parents. It would have given me the new start I needed, and somewhere else to live. I had already got used to taking care of myself and had no fear, because I knew that there was no one else to look out for me or my future in the family. I was going to be eighteen in a few months' time and I knew what my parents had planned for me. I was not shocked, but I had hoped that somehow, in some miraculous way, Papaji might say, "Try for university". I had to accept reality. In more accepting Asian families than mine, university was seen as a way to an independent life for a woman without bringing too much shame on the family, but further education was not an option for many of the women in my community. The fear was that it would make us too independent of the family that we married into. Ambi and I would talk about getting our grades and training in a profession before marriage, because the fear was always that our mothers-in-law − if we had them − might well stop us from pursuing a career. These things propelled us into making sure we studied. Jay and Ambi had quietly continued their studies without encouragement from my parents. As long as their ambitions were not mentioned, this was allowed, with the looming reminder that a marriage would be arranged sooner rather than later. It was now time for me to find another way to leave home.

Instead of going straight home with my A-level results that day, I went for a walk and ended up thinking about my life while sitting on a bench in the park. I watched a little girl swinging just like I had done, dark hair flying and looking as though she didn't have a care in the world. I realised then how much pain everyone suffers and what a lonely journey life can be, yet I didn't understand why it had to be like that. I knew that there had to be a better life than the one my parents had planned for me. I was living in a country where people like me could make free choices, and I could not understand why the choices my family made always seemed to end up in sadness, disappointment and pain. I could not understand (although I had to accept) the fact that my parents were prepared to sacrifice my happiness in order to avoid being criticised by others – this was the worst thing that could happen to them. They cared more for what people thought than for the well-being of their own flesh and blood. It seemed so wrong to me. I wanted to care for the people I loved, I wanted them to be happy too. I could not see how my father could be happy with what had happened to Noor and Jay. I know that he would have been distraught about Ambi and what had happened with her boyfriend. The more I thought about it, the more I knew I could not accept that way of life. It went against everything I believed – there was no compassion, no tolerance, no mercy. I thought about Noor, and Jay and soon Ambi now; they were gone to their marriages, they were no longer a part of our household, and they were restricted in terms of the contact they had with us as much as any contact or visit we had with them. Marriage would mean that I would never go to sleep in the homes of my sisters – the only time that had ever happened was at Noor's when I was a child, with devastating effects on me. Despite everything I missed them, Ambi in particular with the small chats we would have. They were, after all, my family: that never leaves you.

As I sat on the park bench, I looked at the piece of paper in my hand – my grades might not have been good enough for a place at university, but they would get me into nursing. I was ready to do something positive with my life but I would have to go it alone. I stood up. I did not know what was around the corner or what would happen if I made the choice to be free from the restrictions that I was expected to accept; I also knew that there was the risk that my parents would disown me, but I hoped that in time I would gain their acceptance for what I had done and that I could make them proud of my achievements. The girl on the swing looked at me and I smiled at her. *Have courage*, I thought. *Do what you believe to be right.*

I applied, then waited impatiently to hear if I had been accepted to nursing school. I did not mention that I planned to do nursing to my parents or my siblings at this point.

One evening I came in to find both Papaji and Mamaji sitting on the sofa in the lounge, looking serious. I knew something was coming: I was now out of college and soon to be eighteen.

"Sit down and listen," my father said. There was no direct eye contact from either my mother or father. I sat down. "There's a boy, a good Ramgharia, in the Punjab in India at the moment. He's a good match and we'd like you to get married to him as soon as possible." He explained little about how they had arrived at this, whom they had spoken to. The usual secrets that at the point of talking about marriage to your daughter, you should be able to give. Then, as if to add insult to injury he said, "We can't find you a suitable boy from England."

Please, I thought to myself, *don't add the fact that I lack all the specifications and characteristics required of a good Sikh Ramgharia girl and how lucky I am that someone has agreed to take me off your hands.*

I said calmly, "I don't want to marry a boy from India. I live here and I want to work and make something of my life." What I didn't say was, *How could you even think that I would marry a boy who probably doesn't even speak English? How can you do this to me, knowing the pain that my sisters have gone through? How could you imagine that this would be any easier for me than my sisters? Is this really what you think will make you happy?*

My father would not look at me in the eye, could not go against the tradition of purdah that existed even between father and daughter, but his disappointment in me was obvious. It wasn't just the relationship I had had with Kam, although he never mentioned this, it was also the fact that I did not seem to fit into the world that he knew, where women were subservient and never questioned their duties of housework and arranged marriage. Because of his background, his life with his extended family, his limited education. He could only give what he understood that a parent from his background should give. I had been different all along; so many things had set me apart from my family – not just my physical shortcomings which they never ceased to criticise me for, but my keen interest in the outside world which I discovered through school, my own search for spirituality, my wanting to go to college, my love of books. I realised in that moment that he knew how far apart we had grown. And looking at both of them sitting there stiffly, silently, with no emotion on their faces, I also suddenly understood that neither of them cared enough to argue about it; they knew that I would not do something that I didn't feel was right for me. They had always known I was different, but perhaps some part of them always felt that they had not done enough for me. My father was making it clear that he had no appetite for the struggle to bring me back under his control; the problems I had caused (this discussion had come some months after the overdose and Kam; people knew too much) were not of the foremost importance to him, but he just didn't know what else to do. As far as he was concerned, this was my only option, there was nothing else he could offer me; the strain of the financial burdens and the tragedies of his other daughters' marriages had left him exhausted and this half-hearted attempt to marry me off was all he could manage. I didn't blame him for this, and while I knew I had to accept it, it was also very hard for me to understand why he was unable and unwilling to give his unconditional love and support. I left the room and nothing more was said about it.

I spent the next few weeks in a great deal of inner turmoil and conflict. I desperately wanted to do what was right, but it was hard to know what *was* right. I didn't want to hurt my parents and yet what they expected me to do felt so wrong. I beat myself over the idea of leaving them, especially because of their poor health. At the same time I experienced emotional blackmail from my siblings about how much my parents were relying on me to look after them. I so wanted to talk to Ambi about it, to see what her thoughts were about me leaving home but it was impossible. By now she was married and gone, and her duty was to her husband and his family. My access to her, as to my other sisters, was limited; even my parents' visits to her were restricted, and with my reputation and the fear that secrets would be shared when sisters got together, I was obviously not welcome in her in-laws' household so I was rarely invited. It was a family that was notorious for control of the daughters-in-law by the mother-in-law, and disapproval by the father-in-law of anyone who stepped outside of traditions. I knew that my sister was always worried about what restriction they would place on her next.

My two older sisters did not relate to me at all, despite them being my main carers when I was a small child. Ambi was the only one who shared some part of herself with me. I admired her for being brave enough to have had a boyfriend and wondered how she felt, having to give up that love for marriage with a stranger. On the day before Ambi's wedding, I saw her old boyfriend in the car park on the main road near our home. He must have known she was getting married. I told him to go away. Why didn't she have the courage to marry him? He may have been considered low caste but he was still a Sikh, why didn't she take the chance? I think they were very much in love and that he was prepared to do almost anything so they could be together, but she was not. She did not have the courage or the strength to fight against the system. She knew that even though he was a Sikh, he was from a lower caste, so by marrying him she would lose her family. Now she was about to marry a man she didn't even know; she was banking on 'love after marriage' happening, like everyone else. I hoped that she would have that, not like our sisters before her. I had to believe that she would be happy. Would I, could I, take that risk? I had to find a way to leave, and yet still keep my family.

Despite everything, I was afraid of being alone and had no idea how I would cope away from home – I had never been brought up to be anything other than a reliant and subservient wife. Yet I longed for the independence to live a happier life than was being provided for me. Was this so wrong? I would have settled for loving parents, that would have been enough, but I did not feel that I even had this. The gulf between us was so wide that crossing it was a huge risk for them to make and too much for me to hope for. I understood that they were from another world which they tried to hang on to and recreate here in England. They were so far away from the world of seventies Britain in which their children had been raised, a world in which young people like me were exposed to both good and bad influences but at least were allowed to make their own choices. It seemed impossible that they would ever understand me now.

My heart is beating so hard that it feels like it will jump out of my chest and I am so nervous I can hardly breathe. I am standing on the doorstep looking out for a blue car which should be pulling up at the end of our road any minute. My life is about to change forever – have I made the right decision? Suddenly a horn toots and I nearly jump out of my skin. My lift has arrived. As I turn to go back into the house to get my things, I see our nosey Asian neighbour from next door is looking at me. "Sat Sri Akal," I say in greeting, but before she can ask me any questions I grab my bags, close the door behind me and hurry down the street without looking back. I am leaving home.

Chapter 6

Finding My Feet

"Be the change you want to see in the world."

(Mahatma Gandhi)

I had spoken to Pat, my teacher from school, about my situation; we saw each other a few times after I left and she continued to offer me support and guidance. After a long conversation with her in which I told her everything – my wish to do nursing, my parents telling me I had to get married, my fear for my sanity – she agreed that it might be best for me to leave home. I had been accepted for State Registered Nurse training, which would start six months after I left home. She said that I could take my things to her house, which was a few miles away from where we lived, and then I could move in with some friends of hers until things were sorted. The man in the blue car, someone from the shop that I had worked in on Saturdays, kindly offered to take my things to Pat's as I had no one else to help me.

I had only briefly met the people I was to stay with. I took very little and was shown to a room where I stayed for a long time, totally numb. I kept remembering the moment I left home; it went round and round in my mind. I had gone upstairs to fetch the things I had packed and when I came back down with several carrier bags and some clothes still on their hangers, Mamaji was there, watching but saying nothing, no expression on her face. I had arranged to leave during the day, while Papaji was at work, because I feared what he would say and do. I knew that his relatives, especially the men, would not tolerate me dishonouring the family in this way: this would be his main concern. I also feared my siblings' reactions. My brother Dev, who was mostly unknown to me in any real way, would definitely pile the guilt on me. Just before I opened the door to leave, I looked at Mamaji and caught the smallest expression of concern in her eyes, as if she was afraid for herself and what would happen to me as a result of what I was doing.

"I'll be all right," I said.

"Don't do this," she said. "You don't know your father or our relatives, and what they will say or do."

I beat myself up for doing this to her; she was ill, and even though her Parkinson's was more controlled these days, I knew how serious it was. I felt guilty enough, but didn't know what else I could do. At least I would be one less problem for her, no longer a daughter that required tiresome and expensive preparations for the marriage and dowry, which she was always concerned about.

I looked at Mamaji, her small frame, trying to search in her eyes for the 'mother', for some understanding of what life they as parents were prepared to give me. Mamaji still did not know how to respond in any emotional way to me and I had no way of knowing what I should feel for a mother who had not been that mother to me. I wanted her to scream and cry and hold me, and tell me that she loved me and that we could work it out! I knew somehow that she was never able to do this, nor understood that it was normal in the course of life, to fight for your child. I didn't know myself what a mother was – perhaps the closest I got to it was in my teacher Pat, who comforted and consoled me, who listened and talked, who was able to explain right from wrong. I wanted no harm to come to Mamaji, and I hoped that my father's understanding of her illness and compassion for her would prevent any difficulties that she might encounter after today. Even though she was only in her late fifties, she was frail and looked much older. I had cared for her as much as she would allow me to, but her eyes had never looked into mine with love and I had never felt her embrace. I shut the door and fear gripped me.

For days and days, I was racked with the guilt and pain that had been locked for so long in a body that had to survive the harsh realities at home. I cried when I was alone, in bed, until the headache was too painful to continue and I had to breathe slowly to gain composure. I tried to act normally when people were around, tried not to break down; that would not look good. I had learnt not to show my feelings publicly – only Pat had seen these – to hold it together like my family did rather than show emotion; they would let anger spill out instead of 'doing' emotion, and putting an arm around someone would not do. Slowly, I learnt to cry again, like I did when I was a child in India, when the physical beatings didn't matter because the emotional ones hurt more, and in the dark space of the outside toilet in Handsworth, waiting until the threat of physical punishment was over, the emotion contained and the tears swallowed.

I laid quiet for three days after leaving home. I left no address or phone number. My world had been fairly sheltered before now so I did not know how to do many practical things. I'd never even been into Birmingham city centre and had no idea how to navigate my way through this unfamiliar world. I was in a land of shock. All sense of time had gone and I felt that I had cut away part of myself. I was very disorientated, not knowing when one day moved into the next. All sense of time was lost.

Accommodation had been provided but I didn't have anyone to speak to about the situation. There was, unfortunately, some distance between myself and Pat at this time due the birth of her first child. I had continued to have severe headaches and was very anxious. I wondered how my family would react, although I had a pretty good idea, and was embarrassed and shocked on their behalf. I worried about them and their explanations to the others who were so important in their lives. At other times, I wondered if they *were* worried, if they wondered what had happened to me, whether I was dead or alive. I thought this was how parents must feel even if there was no outward expression of emotion about these things from mine. I realise now that Pat may have decided that it was safer not to tell them what she knew or where I was. This was another problem – I did not feel that I could talk to the other women in the house about how I felt, which left me even more isolated. It was different with Pat who seemed to understand about the issues of emotional abuse, control by siblings, arranged marriages and lack of choice. Perhaps at that age I was not really able to explain the complexities of honour and shaming – in fact, it's taken me most of my life to work out how to explain these culturally alien concepts in English.

After three days, I picked up the phone to call home. I could not leave this any longer, had to stop my family being worried about me. I don't know what I was expecting. My mother answered first and spoke briefly, saying that Papaji wanted to talk to me. They both asked where I was and when I would come home. In the end, worn out by the whole experience, I agreed to go and see them.

When I walked into the house my father was there and, from his red eyes, it was obvious he had been crying. My mother was expressionless, but perhaps a little nervous at my visit. This was, after all, out of the realms of her experience; within her familiar world, I had done the unthinkable. My father looked at the floor and said nothing. I said nothing; tears streamed down my face, but my father and I could not look at each other, the curtain of purdah still palpable between us. It was a strange experience, no one saying anything; I knew that somewhere there was the connection between us, the father and child relationship, lost somewhere, but I hoped not forgotten. I knew that I had gone to a place that neither of my parents could go with me. A woman being away from home for several days on her own is not a woman of honour. Whilst I sensed this, and knew that these things were considered wrong, I hoped that my parents could relate to the experiences of the young in Britain, caught between two cultures and affected by them both. Had they both not actually been victims of their own culture? Their relatives dictating how they should do things under the pretence of 'honour'? I stood up and said I had to go, somehow it was up to me now, and no one stopped me, no one tried. I was grateful to be able to do so, but also very sad. There was no discussion, no compromise was suggested, no fight was had to keep me. Yes, even at this point I might have given in to their arms of love, being given permission to say that I had been depressed, that I wanted someone to help me understand what had happened to our family, and ask if there were better choices for me. Was I so selfish to want this? I had indeed done the unthinkable in their eyes. I was sad that even now my parents could not express affection – could we have held each other? Did I have permission to hold them? Still silence engulfed this already vulnerable part of us in this family, a place too hard to go for any of us. Inside I cried, *our family cannot talk.* Not only did I not know what my parents felt about their relationship with me, I did not know what I should feel from their perspective other than the shame that I knew I would bring them, by this act of leaving home. I tried to see this brief visit as reassurance to my already built up fear of possible outcomes and events over the last few days that no harm would come to me if I visited. My family were more worried about their honour, rather than trying to overcome these problems together. The thought crossed my mind that this silence was also familiar because answers to shaming are not possible. I left in a kind of numbness from the whole experience; deep inside I knew that somehow this was the beginning of a very long road of heartache. For now I would not admit that it was possible for my family to deny me. It's what we do as humans when we want to protect ourselves from the possibilities of further rejection. I consoled myself that I would cope better now without the worry of an arranged marriage, without the continued pressures of conformity to traditions that silenced my parents, siblings and other relatives over the years. I would, however, pay for that too.

I phoned home again, some time later, from a kiosk, because I was worried about my family. I was also concerned what people might have been saying to them, because their daughter had left home. My mother answered the phone, and this time Papaji was not at home.

"He says you are no longer his daughter," she said, "and you should hear what the relatives are saying." Mamaji sounded more like an informer than a mother. I reassured myself that she did not know how to handle the conversation with the emotion that was necessary between mother and daughter, but with my already depressed state, it did not stop me going to pieces. This began the cycle of loneliness that I would become familiar with over many decades to come.

I did not know what to say to Mamaji about our relatives. What could I offer that was any consolation for this? I tried to hold on to Mamaji's conversation with me on the phone, but her ability to sustain this was limited: she put the phone down.

I cried uncontrollably all the way back to Pat's friends' house, those all too familiar headaches screaming inside my head. I realised that what I had done had put the family's honour at stake. I was the cause of their shame. If people knew that I had run away, unmarried, my parents would be seen as failures. They might be rejected by their community and stigmatised, and if they didn't shun me, then there was less hope for them in terms of keeping their connections with their close relatives. I was sure that my parents would have told very few people that I'd left home at this stage, but as time went by and it was certain that I would not return, my father would have to tell the wider extended family. I also realised that it would be hard for them to invent suitable explanations for my disappearance and that it would soon be common knowledge. Yet, deep down inside, I felt that the neglect and harm I had suffered at the hands of my family was also shameful. How could my treatment by the family and the little that they had done for me be so easily hidden from people that I was sure may have known about it? I wanted so much to understand.

Back at the teacher's home that I stayed at, my time was taken up with planning for the future. I suffered terrible bouts of loneliness, and continued to feel like a limb had been cut off. I was nervous and anxious and, not surprisingly, unable to explain how I was feeling to people around me. I was so grateful for the accommodation that I received but I had very little contact with Pat as she was tied up with caring for her child. I felt sad about this, but realised that I had to make a life for myself.

Six months after I left home, I began State Registered Nurse training at Hallam Hospital in West Bromwich. I had been accepted and was excited at the prospect of building my life to survive, but also to have something meaningful to give to others. As a group of trainees, some ten of us were offered accommodation at a nurses' home some seven miles away from the hospital. We were ferried between the home and hospital for our shifts in a minibus. We worked long hours and studied very hard. I recall that my uniform had to be taken in to make it smaller and we had paper caps with the number of years' training we had covered marked on them. It was a very busy time, packed with a lot of learning, and you had to be very strong to manage the learning and the work together.

The days that I was off work were, therefore, ones when I felt most alone. They were the times to stand still and think. I remember listening to a lot of music on my first record player. Simon & Garfunkel songs that I wallowed in – *Bridge Over Troubled Water* and *I Am A Rock*, which contains the line "... and a rock feels no pain, and an island never cries". These songs sang the story of my loneliness.

Sometimes I would go shopping and, very rarely, with other nurses on an evening out when they would go to a nightclub. I went along a couple of times after a lot of pressure from them, as I was warned about these places by my peers at Sixth Form. We danced but I would not drink alcohol. I remember thinking that I did not know what the fuss was about, going to these places. I found them smoky and not particularly enjoyable places to be. Perhaps I did not allow myself to relax, sometimes feeling very guilty for doing things that my family would think were wrong. I recall being immensely broken and sad on my days off work.

Once, one of my nursing tutors remarked that my bushy, unruly hair ought to be cut. I wore it tied back but it never quite stayed in place. I decided to take my newfound freedom to the extreme and have it cut at the hairdressers in a more suitable style to hold my nursing cap in place. I knew that if Papaji found out he would never forgive me. Even now, I recall thinking that I was already a Pariah for leaving home as a single unmarried woman, and worried that any decision I made about dress and how I wore my hair could still impact on the family. It would take me a while to be able to feel comfortable in anything other than the trousers we were supposed to wear. As I watched the long dark curls fall to the ground, I knew that this would be considered unforgivable by Sikhs in my wider family who believed that, as God made people with hair, to cut it off would be extremely disrespectful to Him. I did not want to be disrespectful to God, but I also knew that all around me, both Asian and white girls, cut their hair to make it more manageable. My hair once looked like the women's painted in the Pre-Raphaelite art that I had seen! But when the hairdresser had finished, I looked in the mirror and liked what I saw. My hair looked lovely; the stylist had managed to achieve the style which was most popular at that time – shoulder length with the front flicked back in a curl just like Lady Diana, Princess of Wales. The next time I passed my nursing tutor in the hospital grounds, he said, "That's better!" I shyly thanked him. After years of conforming to how girls should dress in my family, I felt liberated. My haircut was also a sign of a change to come, a more independent me. It would take me a very long time to accept and feel comfortable about this independence, though, as my family, culture and religion had been the guiding influence so far. However, I had given myself permission to feel good, at least away from the eyes of my family. Nevertheless, I was terrified of being seen by my father. He had never seen a girl in his family cut her hair. It was hard enough when my brother cut his, but a daughter? I realised many years later that such simple things as cutting your hair were major decisions for me and others like me, because of the way that we had been brought up.

These were strange times for me, and I had to learn to cope with new challenges on my own as there was no one I could talk to about them. I remember the first time I experienced racial abuse. One day on my way back from West Bromwich to Moxley, where the nurses' home was, I walked home through the woods that all the nurses used as a short cut. I was always cautious about my safety, but for some reason, I took this path today, unwisely perhaps, as it was through dense trees and hidden from view, but I was in a hurry to get back to my room. On the way, I passed some young white men who shouted out some racially abusive comments, awful things which shocked and frightened me. I feared that they would target me physically in this isolated area of the woods and I ran away as fast as I could. On arrival at the home, I went to my room and fell on my bed, sobbing. The incident that had just occurred marked for me the isolation from my Asian family, where racial abuse was understood and dealt with by removal of yourself from risks such as those I had just faced. I felt so lost and lonely, empty and rejected. This experience signified the already vulnerable situation I was in, alone. No one at home ever thought of contacting me. I knew it was selfish to want this still, but was I beyond a family that still cared if I was dead or alive? I felt the shock in my mind and body of a lack of compassion from anyone. I also felt let down by Pat; I loved her so much and was unable to understand why she was no longer a part of my life, although now I realise that she had her own family to attend to. My friends Anthea and Baldeep were getting on with their own lives; all the promises that we made in our youth to care for each other were forgotten for now – they too needed to get on with their lives.

I was nineteen years old, doing the stuff of adults in my job as a nurse, but not ready for the independence that I felt I had no choice but to seek. Whilst I had the choice to do whatever I wanted – to go out shopping, get out of bed late on my days off, meet friends – I took no pleasure in doing these things. I did not leave home for a 'good time', as many people in my community would say about their young daughters living independently. I left home to free myself from the limited choices my parents were offering me. I left because being at home was a reminder of my worthlessness, because I did not feel loved, because there was no other choice but to do so. But who would understand this? Who would want to?

I loved what I was doing on the wards, meeting a whole range of people and experiencing 'life'. It was a time to learn and I had a thirst for learning. I felt I was being given a chance to freely learn, just as I had done with Pat at school. I had a mind that enquired and wanted to find out why things worked as they did and how I could do things well.

At the same time, I had to also deal with my identity as I no longer felt part of a family. I was worried that the other Asian girls on my nurse training course might find out what background I came from and the fact that my family had disowned me. There were three on my course, all very different: one had left her husband and was living in the nursing home. She survived through living completely outside her culture and avoiding the others; I could relate to why she needed to protect herself, but we did not connect. The others were supported by their families, one living at home and the other allowed to live away "for the education". However I soon learnt how we all protected ourselves, all three of us actively rejecting arranged marriages. The one who was married was critical of the others living away from home and being independent. It would take me many years to understand why our relationships with our families and culture affected what we could share. Then there was the matter of the guilt I felt. I'd heard people in my community talk of the shame that the girls who 'ran away' brought to the families. I soon learnt that the term 'runaway girls' was a ready label for anyone who sought to exercise their own choice over what their parents wanted for them and was used by Asian and white people alike. It was a term that people I met would use in conversations and I learnt that there were some who would use it to undermine my life. I therefore trusted neither Asian nor white people who did this. I learnt not to share my circumstances with just anyone and began to work out who was genuine and who didn't want to understand but would judge. Guilt was something that I felt often; guilt and then shame, as this was what was often pointed out to me by my siblings. I had brought shame to my parents. Ambi would say, "My in-laws are saying this and that about you." She knew how to make me feel ashamed; she was not telling me this to protect me, she was telling me so that she could continue to toe the line of conformity, a conformity that she herself could not admit was as complex for her as me, as she had chosen not to take my path. At times I felt that she punished me for doing what she didn't feel she could do herself. This would close the little trust that had developed between us.

Whilst in nurse training, I met Elizabeth and Edward, who would go on to become dear friends of mine for many years to come. They were introduced to me by the Church when I left home. Elizabeth and I shared a love of nature and through this we started to communicate; I felt able to confide in her and she became the part-mother that I did not have, offering advice when I most needed it. I believe that Elizabeth and Edward were a godsend and I learnt much from them during my formative years. They helped me get through the difficult times. My emotional state was not good and although I made it to the start of my third year, I finally decided it was best for me to leave nursing altogether. Whilst my time on the course helped me to grow up enormously, I realised that I felt unsupported through the various traumas we had to endure. I sometimes had to leave the ward after we laid out someone who had died. For a long time I lived on stress, whilst still trying to remember that someone else was in a worse situation than me. However, I learnt that I could love people and that this at least was appreciated and valued.

Initially my nursing tutor tried to get me to stay on as I was only a year away from finishing, but she could see that my mind was made up. I had done a psychogeriatric placement in Birmingham. It was some of the toughest care to provide, and as a result I did not feel that my future laid in the physical aspects of care. Instead, the time I had spent on the wards with people, listening to them and counselling them, had brought me to the conclusion that my vocation was in social work. I was now more confident in my skills and eventually my tutor changed her mind and encouraged me. She agreed that doing social work was my desire and the route to the change I wanted to be a part of, especially for young women like me.

But where would I go in between finishing my nurse's training and starting social work? I hated not having a routine. I also didn't want to go on the council housing waiting list, but going home was no longer an option as I had now clearly been disowned. On the rare visits I made to my parents' house I was never welcomed and barely tolerated, in fact they always looked embarrassed, as if they couldn't wait to get rid of me. This was for fear of my being seen by relatives or visitors to the house, as my mother pointed out to me on several occasions. Sometimes she would not let me into the house at all, but would shove a bag full of food into my arms and then close the door in my face. If people thought they'd allowed their wayward daughter back, they would be criticised and made to feel ashamed for being weak. What I had done was so unacceptable in our culture's eyes. I felt enormous sadness that I had no home. I was truly lost in every way. Still, I had prayed that God would "Do whatever He wanted" with me and, sure enough, a friend who I met on the nurse training course said I could stay in their flat in East Anglia and this was exactly the lifeline I needed.

For the next eight months, I divided my time between Birmingham, where I stayed with Elizabeth and Edward and other friends, doing the odd cleaning job here and there to earn money, and using my spare time to prepare for social work training.

I began to relax and enjoy my new surroundings, and felt more confident about my future. One day I was alone in the flat reading when there was a hard rap at the door. I wasn't expecting anyone, in fact no one knew I was there apart from my close friends, and none had arranged to visit. I put down my book and walked quietly to the door. It had a spy hole, so I stood on tiptoes and peered through. It was one of my sisters' husbands! I held my breath and backed away, hoping he would think I wasn't there. He knocked again but eventually I heard him walk away and drive off. It occurred to me that he had come to save my family's honour and take the 'runaway girl' back home. How had he found out where I lived? Maybe my sister had conspired with this. I stopped relaxing after that and was always looking over my shoulder.

At last it was time for me to begin my social work training. My course was at Birmingham University, and I lived in halls of residence at Westhill College, which was originally founded by George Cadbury. The buildings were beautifully designed and were set in a lovely area of green trees where there was plenty of peace and quiet. I was thrilled to be on the course and met a lot of interesting people from different backgrounds. The trouble was that I missed my culture, including speaking in Punjabi, my mother and father and most of all, my siblings, despite their indifference to me. I still wanted to believe that they would one day want to know me and despite their rejection, I still needed to see them. I visited every three or four months and each time the same thing happened: Papaji would go out and Mamaji would sit quietly or ignore me, never expressing any emotion, never asking how I was doing, what I was experiencing or feeling. I think by this stage my siblings were resentful that I should be allowed to visit at all. The distance between my two lives was getting wider and wider. I felt as though I was knocking on the door of someone who didn't want to let me in: I was never welcome. Once, my brother Dev picked me up in his car at Birmingham train station after I'd called home for a lift due to the late time I'd arrived. He clearly did not enjoy collecting me, and kept putting his foot down hard on the accelerator in an attempt to frighten me. He did not talk to me. I felt sorry for him; I wondered what expectations my parents had of him. My mother's illness would have taken a toll on him and he would be expected to keep the family name and honour. I never called home again for a lift.

Although the social work course kept me busy, I continued to suffer the isolation of my situation. I couldn't help noticing the other students being collected by their parents at the end of term. I would return to Elizabeth and Edward or other friends' houses, completely dependent on their kindness and goodwill, and I began to experience real down times. I never recognised it as depression at the time but in later years realised that it must have been. Perhaps I only failed to do so because I was so determined to succeed. The reality was that I feared that if I wasn't determined enough then; there was nowhere for me to go and I would sink. I had to put everything into my studies in order to survive.

While I was doing my training, I had the opportunity to travel to Europe. I went to Dachau concentration camp in Germany which moved me a great deal and made me appreciate how much the Jewish people lost of their families and their history. A trip to France helped me to recognise that Moroccan and other African people I met there had a very difficult time because of racism in European countries. I began to realise how sheltered my upbringing had been. Now, through my experiences in the nursing arena and by talking to people who had been persecuted just because of the colour of their skin, I was gaining a clearer understanding of the world around me. I felt very different to the other students on my course: for a start I was the only Asian woman, and the others' experience was not in the same world as mine. I resisted the culture of drinking and drugs which was present in those days, especially among students, and felt very sidelined because I didn't conform to these social groups. At the same time, I knew that I wasn't the only one with problems, and I wanted to help others where I could. I did a placement with NACRO as well as at a community college and with a social work team. I met many different kinds of situations and people.

After some research and asking around, I was put in touch with two women's organisations that I decided to give a try. The other was a mixture of Asian people in their twenties who met socially to debate issues such as racism in our communities and how this impacted on our lives and our work. My confidence grew from then on as I realised that it was all right to speak out about injustice where this was needed, and that unless people spoke out then change would never come.

However my confidence with my own identity and my family were at their lowest ebb. I wanted things to be right between us but could not see how they would ever accept me. During this time I met an Asian woman on the campus who had an English boyfriend. This was not unusual in the early eighties, although it was unusual to see many Asian students, male or female, at the university even then. She spoke of the difficulties she had with her family not accepting her boyfriend and it was clearly affecting her. I knew then that if there was a way to make that change towards acceptance – not just in Asian communities but in white communities too – then I wanted to be part of that change.

Around that time in the news, there was a case of an Asian woman who had killed her husband. She had suffered from violence and abuse and acted in self-defence, in fear of her own life. For a period I was involved in this campaign. I met some amazing Asian women, articulate and independent. Whenever I spoke to them, it was clear that the majority had parents who supported their independence and they were fully included in family life. This only increased the devastation I felt about my own situation. I longed for my family's support but they continued to shun me, because they had to defend their honour, their izzat, at all costs. A woman living away from home no matter what her age, was not an acceptable situation. During my social work training I came across many Asian women who suffered from sexual abuse and domestic violence. They were brave women who desperately needed support but they always retreated back into their families despite the devastating repercussions for themselves. I didn't want a life like that.

I once did a placement in the Asian community in Sparkbrook and met some lovely young people who welcomed me and included me in their lives. To begin with, I enjoyed taking part in their community events; everything was so familiar to me – the Navratri dances, the music, the food. But then I had a conversation with my placement supervisor who was Asian, and it was clear that he did not like the fact that I had left my family. The idea was completely unacceptable to him. I realised I could not broach this subject within the Asian community. Although I was at last learning about some of the positive aspects of my culture through organising events and attending meetings, I was accepted so long as I didn't mention the isolation from my family. People did not want to know you if you had left home and were a single woman. This was considered wrong – no matter what the reason. As far as most Asian people I came into contact with were concerned, especially those from middle class and professional backgrounds, I was a single, working-class woman who should have conformed to tradition. I was stigmatised and made to feel worthless and it was very difficult not being able to talk about the family I missed so much. Once people knew the truth, maintaining my identity as a Punjabi Indian was very difficult, and yet I could not deny my roots.

The one thing that held me together through these times more than anyone or anything else that I had known was the belief that God knew my identity and I was someone He loved. I also thought about how fortunate I was to have known Pat, Elizabeth, Edward and others such as my girlfriends Baldeep and Anthea at Sixth Form, all of whom had shown me love. I realised that I had to cope alone without them but found it hard to accept that they were not always there for me. I wrote letters and cards to people just to keep me feeling a part of something. I read my Bible as if it was a real person, God, talking to me. I eventually managed to persuade myself that I didn't miss my family any more. I would have to cope, cope with the changes in everything, my culture, identity, race and background. I would have to, but I didn't know how to do it. It was so very hard. By not allowing my family to affect my thoughts, surely I could succeed? I tried, but I never did succeed in not missing them and wanting 'a family'. It would always remain a thought and a hope.

I had learnt from Jay that she was doing a childcare course in Selly Oak. One day I had to go there as part of my social work training so I decided to go and look for her. I was lonely and desperate to see my beautiful sister. This was the only way I could think of to get to see her, as we were not allowed to see each other at home. When I found her, she had just finished for the day and I saw she had my little nephew with her, the oldest of her three children. I was so pleased to see them and walked up to them smiling. My nephew grinned and said hello, but Jay snapped at me.

"You shouldn't have come!" she said, pulling my nephew away. "How did you find me? You know I can't be seen with you." With that she was gone, running for the bus, the lovely nephew who I adored, close beside her, but looking over his shoulder in surprise. I was heartbroken. Jay had never shown much affection towards me, but I had still continued to love her as I had done all the others in the family. I knew that she had been forbidden to have anything to do with me, but I thought she would still have some feelings for me, her baby sister, that she would have given me a hug, a smile, anything but that cold look. She didn't want to know. These feelings were very hard to deal with and it took me a long time to get over that experience.

Chapter 7

Identity Explored, Belonging Explained

"You are the daughter of a king..."

(Jasvinder Sanghera)

I did succeed in some ways. After my social work course finished and I qualified, I was thankful that I had got through this and could finally look forward to a future where I could support myself. I started looking for employment and the first job which appealed, and which I was offered, was as a Youth and Community worker in an Asian youth project in Nottingham. I had not thought about moving from Birmingham, but I also had some very painful memories there and thought that being fifty miles away from home might bring me the peace of mind and new start that I needed. The work was demanding but interesting and I threw myself into it, feeling that I had really found what I wanted to do with my life. I was involved with setting up a number of projects, and making social and recreational provisions for Asian women and girls, most from Muslim, Sikh and Hindu backgrounds, helping to achieve good outcomes for them through community centres, religious organisations and referrals to Women's Aid. I made friends with white women, both lesbian and straight, who volunteered for areas such as Women's Aid and Arts organisations and whose understanding of abused women and genuine offers of help became an important part of my learning process. I also discovered that some of the staff at work (we were all Asian) were going through the same issues with their families as me. I was cautious about what I said because of my earlier experiences of social criticism and I felt it would put me at a disadvantage, and yet I learnt in later years that two of them were in mixed marriages, and one of them was later disowned: there were so many contradictions. I realised that they too had learnt the art of secrecy from their parents, and feared being judged by an all-Asian project team.

For the first time in my life, I was earning money. My salary was good and I saved so that I could afford a home of my own. I was now settling in another town, away from the not-so-good memories of Birmingham. Being physically away from there was a huge relief, as I was always afraid of being seen by extended family on my own, an unmarried woman who had been disowned. I bought a house after renting a flat in Nottingham for six months, and although I was living on my own, it was a fantastic feeling achieving this at twenty four years of age. My work in the Asian youth project opened up all kinds of avenues and opportunities for me to explore different cultures. Whilst I enjoyed this, there were also challenges in finding my feet as the new me. I began networking and met people from diverse backgrounds who were talented in all kinds of areas.

I still found it hard to move on from my family's rejection and the stigma of disownment, but I was glad to be busy and helping solve other people's problems, as it took my mind off my own. Contact with family was minimal: phone calls were not real calls, a word or two from me to my mother who did not know what to say. If my brother answered he always passed the phone to my mother and my father would not talk to me at all. If he answered, the phone would be dropped and left for my mother to pick up. It was as if they just needed to know that I was living and no more. Ambi called one day.

"Mum and Dad say you can't come home any more, they can't do anything for you," she said.

I couldn't understand why she felt she needed to say this to me when I knew it anyway. I did not respond to her comments, or even try to explain what was happening to me. Ambi did not want me to explain, she did not want to hear of how the situation was psychologically affecting me. She was angry at life, but would not let me in. I consoled myself by saying that it was too painful for her to deal with, but when I didn't hear from her, or she talked about events in her life that I could have no part of – being too busy in her job, a house move, children and the things that affect us all in so many ways – I began to feel very insecure; bouts of depression and anxiety consumed me. As ever, I felt totally abandoned. I could not think of losing the little contact I had with her and was desperate to keep a connection with her, as she was the only one from whom I had the occasional letter or had a phone conversation with. I refused to recognise the pain she could cause because I could not afford to.

In letters, she told me, "I am not happy because Mum and Dad didn't do enough for you."

But she never mentioned whether she had stood up for me, or if she even tried. She stated the facts in a cold, cruel way. I often wondered if she treated me this way because this was how she was used to being treated.

I remember one strange situation: Ambi set up an introduction for me with a young Ramgharia man in France; this went terribly wrong. I didn't fully understand what was going on but turned up at the appointed place in Paris and had to spend two very uncomfortable days with people I clearly had nothing in common with and knew I could not get on with. It was a nightmare trying to get out of it and I was so glad when the time came for me to go home. I was naïve to trust her, but I wanted acceptance from her and the family. Perhaps she thought she was helping me by trying to arrange a suitable match, or perhaps she was under pressure from her in-laws to do so. I never found out. Things got even worse when the man in question said some unpleasant things about me – presumably because I turned him down – and I resolved to be more careful in future and listen to my instincts. I am glad I did.

One day, my friend Liz, who was also a youth worker, asked if I would like to go to India with her. I thought about it and decided that this was a chance to find out who I really was. I remembered my early childhood there and the sadness, but also the Punjab as I had felt it; maybe the villagers would remember me and maybe my Pooha, my father's sister, would see me differently to the way my relatives and extended family in England did. I decided that this was a chance for me to link with the past, to seek some answers. Perhaps it would help me to move on. By this time, I had started a new job, still in Nottingham but now setting up women's training schemes, doing research and working with women on life skills programmes and supporting them through non-traditional skills training.

Whilst making plans for my trip to India, in June 1985, I met Philip. I was introduced to him through a dating agency (and there were very few such agencies back then). I had begun to realise that in the circles I found myself, I would not be meeting many Asian men who would be serious about a relationship leading to marriage. Caste, clan and religion were not criteria I would easily meet in a relationship and I still held onto my Christian belief and values in life. In my dating advert, I had to say what kind of man I wanted to meet, and so I ticked the boxes for both Asian and white men. I felt my choices were going to be limited so it seemed to be the best option. It felt strange to be potentially 'arranging' my own marriage, although at this stage I had no idea how meeting someone this way would work out. Neither of us had met anyone else in this way before, and we were both very cautious, if not a little shy. Philip called me by telephone first, and after speaking on the phone many times and getting on well, we agreed to meet in Loughborough after I had been to visit a friend there one weekend. We chose to walk around Carillon Park – a place that was familiar to both of us. It was a warm Sunday afternoon in June, and families were out and about enjoying the sunshine. Despite us talking and getting to know each other beforehand, we were very nervous; I was cautious but talkative. He was a lovely person, very respectful with a gentle quality that I rarely saw in others. We didn't think about our differences, we only saw each other for the people we were. Philip would later say that he thought that I was checking him out to see if he believed in equality and yes, perhaps racism had been a fear and something I had experienced and acknowledged. We arranged to meet again, this time at Leicester railway station, as I was passing through from Birmingham to Nottingham. I worried that my family's reaction on hearing about this relationship with someone not just outside my clan but of a different race would have far-reaching consequences, and knew that it was another reason for my family to further disown me. I only had minimal contact with them at this time: things were still strained and each time I saw them I ended up in turmoil. It would take me ages to get back on my feet again after a visit and I would throw my nervous energy into work and more work.

When I got into the car, Philip greeted me with a shy smile. We sat for a minute, then I said, "I don't know if we should see each other again." Even as I said it, I was kicking myself for being so heartless; I liked him, but my own insecurities about the family and my own low self-esteem all got in the way. Philip looked concerned; there was silence, then he said that he thought that we might have a chance, and that he felt we had left our last meeting on a positive note. I realised as he spoke that I wasn't giving him, or myself, a chance. There were tears in his eyes, he was a genuine person and I had no right to dash his or my feelings so readily. After this, Philip and I saw each other regularly, building a meaningful and close relationship based on love, trust and respect.

In November, I went to India as planned with my friend Liz. I hated leaving Philip; we had a farewell dinner and he made jokes about me meeting a Maharajah in India. There was clearly no chance of that, I knew! However, Philip was deadly serious underneath, I think, that I might meet someone there for marriage. I realised that I was far too much in love with him to consider a future without him, and I didn't need to go to India to know what a fool I would be to give him up.

I love India from the moment the plane touches down. We have an amazing journey, staying in budget hotels, travelling through changing climates to Delhi, making our way further north to the Himalayas where we see some incredible sunsets, then heading down to Jaipur in the south and Ajmeer. I see palaces but no Maharajahs, and cows on the streets, rather than elephants with princes on their backs. Now, I sit on the rickety bus to the Punjab on the famous Grand Trunk Road. My father has written to his sister, my Pooha, to say that I will be arriving some time in November. At first, I was amazed that my father did this for me but now I realise that he had to, because what would people say in his home village if his daughter, a single woman, turns up alone and unchaperoned by a man. I am grateful, nevertheless. As we approach the Punjab, my heart beats faster and then tears begin to roll down my cheeks. It feels like I'm coming home. I am also crying for a past left behind, a past that might have been less traumatic if my parents had never migrated but where, in my imagination, I would have had to accept things as they were done in India. I lean my forehead against the window and watch the landscape stretching away in the distance, familiar and strange at the same time. Here are the lush green fields which I loved so much, people toiling over them, in some places buffalo still being the only power available to cultivate the land. Through the window, I feel the easy warm air blowing in, beckoning me to touch Mother Earth. People live much closer to nature here and have a great respect for the land and what it provides; they feel a strong connection to it. Here, my parents and generations before them worked hard every day to provide enough for their families. I remember my mother trying to grow vegetables in the cool British climate and poor soil – radishes, onions, lettuces and spinach (as well as my favourite marigolds) – as though she could not lose that connection with the earth even though she was so far from home. I taste the salt on my lips. *The Punjab is still a part of me*, I think. I am surprised at my feelings but know that they are natural. Yet I also know that I no longer belong in the India that I knew or the Africa where I was born, or the England of my parents where I am not accepted. So where do I belong? Who am I?

We get off the bus and start walking down the rough and stony road towards the village – where generations of my paternal family have lived. It is extremely hot even though it's November. We soon pass a few houses and I begin to remember things from all those years ago; I know that 'my' house is not far up on the left hand side at the edge of the village. It is very quiet; the sun is at its hottest and most people will be inside, trying to sleep until it cools down. The houses are tall concrete buildings and cast welcome shade; we stop for a moment, putting down our heavy backpacks. I am finding it hard to speak. After all this time, after all these miles, here I am, back in my childhood home. I have a mixture of feelings; I wonder what it was like for Mamaji to return after so many years away in exile. We all experienced feelings of sadness and abandonment during those years and it must have been hard for my mother as a lone woman with her children, living in the village without a man to uphold her honour and having to do everything herself. I knew there were relatives living nearby, but they were not people that my parents relied on as much as the kin in East Africa. How did she really feel about it all?

I am jolted out of my thoughts by a man who approaches and asks what we are doing. I explain that I have come to see my Pooha, my paternal aunt; he leads us to the house and tells us to wait outside. When he comes out, he says that my aunt has gone to the fields and he will go and fetch her. I look at the house; it is a tall yellow building, but not as tall as I remember — when I was little I thought it was enormous. The sandy path leading to the house is the same: I remember playing there and then running home to wash the dust off my face under the 'Nalka', or water pump. I look around and notice the pharmacy where a man is

150

standing with his arms behind his back, looking at us intently. Then my Pooha arrives, hands full of vegetables and a long scarf thrown over her head in a gesture of respect for a guest. When she sees me and recognises who I am, she comes forwards, puts out her arms and hugs me, just as I imagined she would. We both cry, feeling that connection with my father, her brother. Her hug tells me that I am family and it means a great deal to me.

Pooha and her family are now caring for the house. I meet Harpreet, the youngest of her sons. There are two sons remaining in Chachrari, the others are in England, married and settled. Pooha takes care of me as a mother would do; she treats me with respect, she talks of missing my father. She remembers me as a small child. I remember her look, her build (she is slim like Ambi), her face not unlike my father's with high cheekbones, deep-set eyes and a broad smile. I am here for two weeks before returning to England. I do everything I need to: visit my old primary school, still in the open, taking pictures of the teacher and class. Is it really nineteen years since I stood here, my whole life ahead of me? There is little change. The teachers are curious and children look at us with wide eyes; they know I am from England, despite my traditional Punjabi dress. I am welcomed by the neighbours; there is no toilet in our house so I have to go to theirs, each time having to pass the fierce dog at the gate. Massi, the neighbour, is the one who recalls my two older sisters, the beatings, me screaming. "I told them to stop hitting you…your crying could be heard a lot of the time," she says. I am surprised that she remembers from so long ago but I am also transported to the sadness of that time for me and the family.

As Liz has decided to go on to Shrinigar, we see Diwali in the village before she goes. Diwali is the festival of lights for Hindus and Sikhs. It celebrates the victory of good over evil and light over darkness, the triumph of hope over despair. It marks a new beginning, a renewal of commitment to family values, and represents all the good virtues we seek such as love, reflection, forgiveness and knowledge. It is a very sociable time when families visit one another, share food (samosas and sweets, either homemade or bought from the sweet maker's shop) and let off fireworks in the streets. As we walk through the village in the darkness, we see candles flickering on the rooftops and lighting up every room in the house to celebrate the good news.

I visit the Golden Temple in Amritsar and cry at the thought of my father's deep desire to be here, to undertake the Sikh pilgrimage which he has done many times before. As a devout Sikh, he lives for his faith despite his worries and shortfalls. I visit Guriya and Phagwara and buy food at the street stalls, marvelling at the range of delicacies being crunched and swallowed: fresh matai and crispy golgappas. More than anything, it is the sight of the house my father built that moves me, even though it, and the road it is on, are smaller than I remembered, such is the memory of a child. I walk around the house, it is built in the basic, traditional style of over a hundred years ago, yet the workmanship is very clever and there is art and design in evidence around the courtyard. I climb to the rooftop and close my eyes, remembering the times when us girls came up here to dry our hair in the hot sun. I look down and see a cow in the garden; they still make firewood from the cow dung. I watch women gather together in the morning for their toileting walk. Women are not allowed to go out at certain times: there is still tension and worry as the storming of the Golden Temple has not long passed.

There is nothing more touching or memorable than the visit to my mother's village. Here we meet my uncle, my mother's brother. His father, my grandfather, was a musician and he is an artist, a sensitive man, very small like me and my mother, no more than five feet tall. He shows me a painting he has done depicting Layla and Majnun, and I marvel at its beauty. It depicts a scene from a famous love story between a rich girl, Layla and a poor boy, Majnun, also known as the Madman. When Layla's parents find out, they force her to marry someone else but Layla cannot bear the thought of being separated from her lover and commits suicide. Hearing this news, Majnun goes to the graveyard where his sweetheart is buried and kills himself. It is amazing to see this gorgeous painting taking pride of place in the lounge of his small house in this rugged village. I suddenly remember that we used to have some of his paintings in our house in England; they were quite often painted on wood, not canvas, as this was all he had, and many were of Indian gazelles, leaping in the wild. I don't think the rest of the family appreciated them as much as I did. They were kept in the loft of the house.

He takes me to my mother's old home at my request. We see the house where she lived with the whole of her family before that. I am saddened by the conditions that she had to contend with – it is like going into a dark cave; the roof of the house is low and there are tunnel-like passages to tiny rooms. The walls are like moulded caves. It is beautiful in its simplicity. The kitchen particularly affects me. My mother would have had to crouch on the floor to cook in this tiny space; the floor and walls are cement and red stone. The simplicity is like the pictures I have seen depicted in some Bibles, of houses in the time of Jesus. I shed a tear for my mother, a woman who could not always embrace me or see me with compassion but who had so little compassion offered to her. Her life in this tiny house must have been very difficult: cooking, cleaning, milking cows, making butter, grinding flour and corn, preparing the dung for firewood and so on. She would never have rested. This would have started when she was very young and gone on until she left to marry my father. I begin to understand the sadness that she must have felt for not having the basic right to attend school, to never think of herself because her blind mother and brothers and father saw her as necessary for meeting their needs, as was the case for most of the women around her.

On my return from Pasla, I return to Pooha's care with compassion for her and the women that I meet in the village, for their lives too are difficult. Although some of the houses have TVs and gadgets that make life easier, my Pooha has not. That night I lie in my sleeping bag in the front room, watching the foot long lizards which camouflage with the acid green on the walls. I miss Philip and am ready to go back home, and I am thankful to my Pooha for being the mother she has been. There are tears on my farewell as a taxi arrives to collect me and take me to Delhi. Some of the villagers have come to say goodbye. Although I saw poverty on my arrival and the struggle for life in the village, on my return home I remember people rich with laughter and joy for life too, people who did not judge me for my visit as a woman alone. Although I know that I have come as someone does for a holiday, for me it has been more than this, an exploration into the past and it has been what I have needed to understand my parents' history as an adult, and why they were the people they were. It has surprised me because during this time I have also felt more assured about the goodness and sincerity in my relationship with Philip.

Chapter 8

An Honourable Marriage, Joy and Turbulence

"All marriages are mixed marriages."

(Chantal Saperstein)

When I arrived back in England, Philip was waiting for me with open arms and it felt wonderful to be with him again. I had feared the family's possible reaction to my relationship with him but knew now that I could not let go of something that felt so right. I realised that being with Philip was no more wrong than being with someone that my parents wanted to match me with so long as we were all in agreement that this was the right person for me. Philip treated me with more love and respect than anyone I had ever known. As we had both grown up in Britain during the 1960s and 1970s, we shared similar values: we had respect for people from multi-racial communities and we both had friends from a variety of backgrounds. We found common ground through the values of our Christian faith and we also had similar educational experiences through diverse schooling and university. I asked myself, *Is it so wrong that I should want to remain connected to this man? A man who is keen to learn about my Sikh family roots so that he might understand me better, and my family too?*

On my return from India, my understanding of my cultural roots and identity were very different to how they had been prior to visiting the Punjab. Whilst there, I saw and spoke to many ordinary people; I was able to ask them about the things they valued and what was important to them in life. It seemed that whilst day-to-day survival in practical terms was high on the agenda, their love, respect and care of each other was also just as important. This was shown in their inclusion of me as if I was part of their family, I was treated no less. I brought that back with me, feeling more certain that this is what family and identity meant.

By then I also understood more about the fear that some families have of their children marrying outside the community, but was convinced that men and women had the right to choose to be with someone that was the right match for them as an individual person, taking into account their personality, needs and happiness. Why should it matter if that person was not from the same background, especially if they were prepared to embrace the culture of the new family? I had heard all the arguments about why marrying out of race or culture was wrong, which included 'irreconcilable' religious differences and even more extreme racist ideas, which I found shocking. I would ask people whether life was so predictable that they could never imagine themselves in a mixed relationship. I talked about the fact that mixed couples and mixed communities were here to stay and could contribute a huge amount to the debate of equality, showing that it was possible to love your neighbour no matter what your background or ideals.

I had spent a great deal of time thinking about all this whilst in India and talked about it with Philip when I came home, discussing it over a period of many weeks. Despite the potential difficulties ahead, Philip and I were more certain than ever that it was the right thing for us to be married. We knew that prejudice existed towards mixed couples, we were not naïve about this, but we also knew that it was becoming more and more acceptable in Britain for Asian and other racial groups to be intermarried, and we were prepared for any challenge to that and felt sure that as long as people met us and knew what this meant to us, they would see our commitment to each other and realise that you do not have to look alike to make a marriage work.

We talked about it and agreed that we would try to get the blessing of my family in the hope of putting an end to all those years of isolation and heartache. We wanted them to accept Philip and, although we knew what a challenge it might be to convince them, we thought that given time it could all work out.

I did not know how I was going to introduce Philip to my family and decided to start with Ambi initially to test the situation, as I hoped that she would tell me how my family might respond. She and I had little contact at that time, and what there was had to be secretive on her part due to her in-laws' disapproval of me and the independence that I sought to live and work away from home. I had only the phone to get in touch with her and did not know her address — such was the disownment of a sister realised. She lived up north with her husband and young daughter, and although I could tell she was nervous about the idea, she agreed to meet Philip and me and said that her husband would also be present. I can only imagine that she realised I had been to India and that I had thought about what I was doing. I was pleased that she accepted my request as she had not been so generous in the past. Years had gone by, almost eight in total, I knew little about her life, and she knew even less about mine.

On arrival up north when Philip and I visited, we had a light-hearted meal with the odd nervous laugh from her husband but I had my hopes up high. I was now able to work, look after myself and had a steady job. Philip was in a good job too. Having realised that I wanted to spend the rest of my life with Philip, I had taken the first step towards him being accepted by my family through this meeting with my sibling.

Some days after the visit with Ambi, I telephoned her. To my surprise, she began to question me.

"Why do you have to marry a white man?" she asked. "Mum and Dad won't be happy about that. People in the community will talk." I suddenly wasn't so sure that I had Ambi's support. She told me that her husband didn't like the idea and her in-laws certainly wouldn't if they found out. I decided not to ask her for help in telling my parents and she didn't offer. I understood that she had a difficult situation with her in-laws and I didn't want to lose her by asking her to do something that might cause her problems. I loved Ambi and she was the only one left in my family that I could talk to.

By December 1986, Philip and I had bought a house together and were busy planning the wedding. The invitations were almost ready and of course we talked about whether my family would come. In the end we decided that I would go to Birmingham and talk to my parents, to see if they would listen. Philip and I had spent many, many hours talking about the situation with my family. He tried to understand, but I realised that he had not come across this kind of situation before: still, he remained optimistic and hoped for my sake that things would work out. The journey was nerve-wracking but I decided that I had nothing to lose after so much heartache with my family over the years. Philip parked the car some distance away and left me to go and break the news alone. We knew that there was every possibility that I would be permanently disowned and that I would never see any of my family again. I was marrying not only out of the clan but out of my race too, to a white man. I had been tolerated from afar for the last eight years and seen a handful of times but never accepted back into the fold, but this could possibly result in complete separation.

Mamaji was home; she told me that Papaji was in the garage doing carpentry. Mamaji's health was not too bad at this time – her illness was controlled well, but she was, as usual, not focused.

"I want to speak to you," I said, not knowing even now, as a twenty six year old woman, how to speak to her, what to say. We sat down. I was paralysed for a while. I asked about normal things: the garden and the vegetables that she grew; she spoke of her health and how she couldn't do so much now. She didn't ask anything about the life that I was living, she knew I had my own home and a job and that was it. The few things we talked about in these exchanges of words were familiar. She mentioned money, saying that if I was earning I could send some home for her to save. It only confirmed my belief that to her I was just a potential commodity and I felt I owed them nothing after nine years of struggle, having to look after myself without any particular support that I could well have done with over this time. In the silence between us, I wondered if she really could not see me as a daughter, her own flesh and blood. Did she not care how I felt, missing her and the family? Did she not understand how hard it was to be treated this way and to be disowned? My understanding of her after my trip to India made it so hard to see why she could not accept my wish to move on with a better life. Finally I came out with it:

"Mamaji, I want to get married. I have met someone – Philip. And yes, he is an Englishman…"

For a moment, her eyes looked directly into mine and her hands shook a little. I felt for her. I knew it was stupid of me to think that she might be happy for me, but I couldn't help but hope.

"Acha (yes)," she said finally, as if resigned. "But you must not tell your father, do you hear me? Please don't tell your father."

She pleaded with me not to tell Papaji a number of times. Despite my certainty in my choice of Philip, I understood my mother's fear because she would have to be the one who told him the bad news which would eventually find its way out to the wider family. She would have to deal with his anger and shame. I had known deep down that this would not be acceptable to Papaji, and certainly not to his relatives. My mother's reaction made it clear that I was right. My father would be furious with the choice I had made. I had already done the unthinkable in many things to them, and now this.

"Challa ja! (Go)" my mother shouted suddenly, making me jump. "Go, and don't come back here, do what you want, marry him. It's fine with me because we can't do anything else for you!"

With those words, I knew she was disowning me for the umpteenth time but it was no easier for me. I would have to be less than human not to feel the pain and devastation of this. I even felt that I ought to be able to handle this in the way my family expected me to, but I could not. I started shaking, still the vulnerable child which my mother had never protected. I realised that my sisters had trained me well, to take responsibility for all my parents' needs, their health, their happiness and their honour – how could I destroy this in one fell swoop of a decision for myself? *I am selfish, I am a bad person, I deserve to be rejected and disowned,* I thought. Perhaps I should ask my family what I should do. It occurred to me that I would never have an answer from them; my family's silence had shown me that I was worth nothing. On my return home, these events took their toll, but I knew that I had to move on with my life. This was a chance of happiness for me and Philip.

So Philip and I continued to prepare for our wedding. We sent invitations to my parents, to Ambi, her husband and her seven year old daughter, and to a cousin in Nottingham who was a free-thinking Sikh. We received no replies.

There were hearts and bells — colourful confetti fluttering in the breeze and drifting onto the grass outside Newstead Abbey. It was a chilly February day: Elizabeth put a cardigan around my shoulders. I was wearing a cotton and lace white wedding dress and carrying a bouquet of red and white flowers; there were red roses for the men's buttonholes too, since red is the colour of luck and is almost always worn at Indian weddings. My cold hand linked with Philip's warm one, he looked straight into my eyes and smiled: we were very happy. The year was 1987, I was twenty seven years old and it was almost ten years since I was first disowned by my family.

On the wedding day, my brother, who still lived with my parents, came to the registry office with Ambi, her husband and child. I was surprised and confused but so grateful to them for being there and let them know this. The day went very quickly. I remember a serious-looking Ambi in a yellow chiffon sari staring at the table as Edward and Elizabeth made the speeches. I really didn't know my brother in any significant way (our relationship was dictated by his loyalty to the clan and what my parents said), and I wondered if he had been sent by Papaji as a sign of wishing me well, or maybe guilt – I am still not sure. My father had sent £101 tied with a red wedding thread. I was touched but wondered what it meant. For a moment I felt hopeful again, that this could be a gesture of reconciliation. It was the most hope I had ever had but I was also fearful that this could also be the last contact, the last straw. Was this a closure for the family, played out in some weird drama? There were some jokes between my brother and other guests, but my family all left early. Still, we had a wonderful day. As I fell asleep, I was happy for the start of my new life but aware of a shadow I could not deny. I had married outside my family, my clan and my culture and although it was never said to me directly, I had heard enough conversations to know that with a few exceptions, my father had a low opinion of the British because of what he had seen during the time of the Raj. By marrying a white man, I had given my parents even more reason to be ashamed; now I would have to pay the price.

After the wedding, there were lengthy silences from Ambi and the rest of my family. I was constantly reminded of my disownment and lived in perpetual uncertainty about whether this time it was permanent. I decided to give everyone time to settle and waited several months before I rang home. My brother would not speak to me, and passed the phone to Mamaji who told me I shouldn't have called as my father was home. Another time Mamaji said, "Your father said you are no longer his daughter."

She told me that Papaji's brother and his nephew disapproved and had told him not to have any contact with me any more. She kept repeating that my father had disowned me. The message was loud and clear but I was unable to accept it. Papaji never said he disowned me to my face; the message was only passed on through my mother and Ambi. That was the way it was, the children and mothers kept the honour of the father, and he did not have to see me or be answerable for his actions.

In April 1987, I had an ectopic pregnancy. Luckily it was caught in the early stages, but a whole fallopian tube had to be removed in emergency surgery. I was devastated by the possibility that I would never be able to have children and felt very alone. I made attempts to speak to Ambi, hoping that she would agree to see me, wishing that she would reach out to me at this time of need. The only family I had now was my husband and I wanted the comfort of a woman, a sister, someone who understood what I was going through. But it was not to be. Whenever I phoned her, it felt like I was approaching a stranger, someone who could not engage on this intimate level. I did not even know if she told my mother or siblings about the operation, and to this day I still don't. She showed no compassion at this time. Despite her coldness, I continued to try to contact her, although I would leave a space of weeks – months at times – as conversations with her were very difficult. When I did manage to speak to her, she was so angry; anger that I did not think possible in a sister. Instead of us finding middle ground she was judgemental of my actions. I found it so difficult to accept that my own flesh and blood showed no warmth towards me and the pain of rejection was hard to cope with. I'd had so much of it that I was by now very nervous about any contact I had with Ambi, as each time we spoke I would end up feeling shattered. I realised that the situation with her was like fighting against a harsh wind, yet despite my trials I continued to fight to be part of her life and, through her, part of my family's life. I would try to move on then make another attempt to contact her; each time, any glimmer of hope would be cruelly dashed, but still I could not give up. I longed for this natural acceptance. I sometimes wondered if I was being naïve in thinking that I could change the fact that disownment was inevitable for anyone who did what I did: I had stood up for what I believed to be right and had known the consequences when I left home. These thoughts and doubts would consume me and guilt would ensue. I wondered if Ambi wanted me to say sorry for marrying out, for leaving home, for thinking independently, for doing the things that any child might do when I was younger, seeing Kam, or wanting to read my Bible. Would Ambi accept me any more if I broke down and pleaded on my knees? But I could not be who she wanted me to be. Redemption was not possible.

"Please tell me what you think I should do," I'd asked her the last time we spoke.

"I'll tell you what my husband says you should do. He says you should leave Philip and return to the family. That's the only way you'll ever be accepted back."

This was the husband who had come to my wedding with his wife and child; what had changed between then and now? The pressure from his parents? Or perhaps a dislike of his sister-in-law's independence? I thought it was probably the latter, it was clear that he disapproved of me from his lack of interaction with me. If he loved her, he would have allowed her to have a relationship with me, her sibling, and could have helped bring the families back together. I thought about it almost all the time: the longing would never go away. All I really knew was that my sister's loyalty was not to me. Was it too tall an order for her? Could she not continue to have a relationship with me without her family knowing? Ambi had already played the game of secrecy with me in her first relationship: was it too much for her to see me in this way now? I realised that I would have accepted anything, because I so feared having no connection with my family at all.

I tried to reason with her to find a way through; at the same time, my grief was so great, having lost her and the rest of the family as well as having the ectopic. She could not see how this affected me psychologically and how depressed I was. She was never able to engage in this process. She accused me of having been "Westernised" and not recognising that I had done wrong. I wonder now if she was angry with me because she was angry with herself and I had made choices that she would like to have made. It felt as though the more she knew about my vulnerability, the harder she pushed in attack. I felt defeated all the time. I found it so hard to accept that someone could be rejected by their family for doing what I did. I was surrounded by people who were themselves in difficult situations but who worked at their differences and found reconciliation and forgiveness; but I would never be forgiven. I was being punished for a matter of honour and as far as Ambi was concerned, I deserved everything I got.

One evening in October 1987, Philip answered the telephone. It was my brother Dev and he wanted to speak to me. I couldn't think why or what it could be about. He was still living with my parents as far as I knew, so I wondered if one of them was ill: I'd had no communication with them since my marriage as it was clear that I was not welcome at home.

I walked over to Philip with a questioning look and he passed me the phone.

"Hello? Dev? What's…?"

He cut me off in a rough voice. "Papaji died of a heart attack three days ago," he said. "I'm just phoning to tell you about the funeral."

I couldn't speak, I just gripped the phone and listened. He told me in no uncertain terms that if I tried to bring my husband with me to the service at the crematorium, my sisters' husbands would prevent him from entering. He told me that people, relatives within the community, were saying that I had killed my father because I had caused him stress by leaving home and marrying a white man. Before I could respond, he hung up. I looked at Philip trying to make sense of what I had heard and felt like I had fallen through a hole in the floor.

The week before the funeral was one of the most difficult that I can remember in my life; I didn't know what to do or say to anyone. I had not been invited by my brother to come home: my family would all be there and he was clear that I could only come to the funeral. My siblings did not call me, nor did my mother. I desperately wanted to speak to her, yet I was not sure I could take what I knew she was bound to say: "Don't come to the house, don't shame us." I feared everything in the situation that was possible.

I remember thinking that my father was the only one in my family who I held in such high esteem, despite his distant and sometimes strange relationship with me. This esteem came in part from being head of the household as was the norm in most Sikh families, but he was not overbearing: he loved us and treated us well. This was shown through his gestures, but not always verbally. I tried to think of what he did for me, but it was hard: we were estranged from each other and at this time, knowing that I would never be able to ask him the questions I so wanted the answers to, it was even harder to find the sense of that relationship. All that I could say was that I had loved him and would continue to even after his death.

As I dressed for my Papaji's funeral, my heart was as heavy as lead. Now all hope of ever seeing him again was gone, and I had not even been allowed to say goodbye. I tried to remember the last time I saw or spoke to him – it must have been not long after I left home when I was eighteen, ten years ago. All I had had from him was the ambiguous acknowledgement of my marriage to Philip, when Dev handed me £101 tied in a red thread and told me it was from Papaji. Surely the gift was not the action of someone who hated me? Could my choices really have stressed my father enough to kill him? I knew this was his third heart attack; he had had two whilst I was living at home during my teenage years. I did not know how to grieve; I was in shock, but without any information about what had happened to my father – how he had died, what his last days had been like – I did not know what to think or feel. There was no one I could talk to apart from Philip, but I could not explain to him the impact of the words that were going round and round in my head. *"You killed Dad…"*

I knew that it would be very difficult to face my family – and everyone else from the community – at the funeral, but nothing would stop me saying this last farewell to the father I had always loved. I was supposed to go with my friend Shan, who had offered to accompany me for moral support. Philip took me by car to the gates of the crematorium and left me there to wait for Shan, but she didn't turn up. I wasn't sure what to do but after a while, with great trepidation, I made my way into the crematorium. The room was full of several hundred people: all I could see were the heads of women in white chunnis and men in their white turbans and there was a respectful silence. Almost everyone was seated and I was directed to some benches at the back. I looked for my family, but they were all at the front beside my father's coffin; it was pine with gold handles. I saw my aunt, my Bhabhi, sitting with them. I remembered her from my childhood; she was always interested and warm. When she turned round and saw me, she stood up and came over.

"You need to see your father," she said with some urgency, but softly. My aunt was an understanding Sikh woman. She knew that it was easier to grieve and accept that someone had died if you saw their face and said goodbye to them. She went up to my family and begged them to bring me forward to be with them, but her words fell on deaf ears. They took a brief look at me and then turned their faces away. My aunt complained under her breath that I should see my father, it was part of his culture and religious expectations; her attempt was brave, but ignored. Seeing my father never happened — even now at this time, the family would not allow it, and yet it is a thing all Sikhs are supposed to do.

I was very affected by the atmosphere in the room, knowing that all these people had come to pay their respects to my father, that they were grieving too. But the worst thing was that they knew how and why my father had died: I was still desperate for the answers. The fear of what the people there thought of me consumed me and my throat tightened. My brother Dev's words echoed sharply in my mind. *"People are saying you killed your father..."* The service started and the priest recited the Sikh prayers I was so familiar with. The coffin drew up on the belt and there was a gasp from some of the mourners. I held back my tears but inside I was crying for what I did not know about my Papaji, what had happened to him; despite everything he was still my father, and I still loved him. My sisters didn't turn their heads to look at me, nor did my brother. As the funeral ended, people went outside to see my father's smoke released into the air. I waited for one of my siblings to invite me back to the Gurdwara where there would be prayers and comfort but they ignored me. In the end, a distant relative asked me to accompany her and I followed with a heavy heart. Even then I hoped for some compassion and to be able to join my family in the grieving but I was sadly mistaken. Dev, as well as Noor, Jay, Ambi and their respective husbands and children – the very large family that had now extended – stayed far out of sight. Even in our grief, we had no connection. Later in the Gurdwara – where I found my friend Shan who had arrived late – I saw Mamaji sitting on a chair, a few people around her, mostly women. Nearby the Langar were being prepared in the Gurdwara kitchens: the familiar smell of food and the generosity of the Sikhs warmed my heart. Eventually my mother saw me; her face was thin and pale and it looked as though half of her life had gone. Her hands, in slow motion, rose to her face.

"Your father has gone," she whispered. She obviously felt that she had to tell me this as a parent, but that was all she had to say. I reached out and hugged her but there seemed to be no connection between us. It lasted only a few seconds, then she pushed me away and continued talking to the others. I never dreamed that my mother would be unable to reach me at such a time, that I would not be accepted at my own father's funeral. As I watched her, I reminded myself that I had to take my place as a disowned daughter, and that my mother would expect me to. The events of this time affected me greatly over a number of years.

Not long after the funeral, in May 1988, I started a new job as a social worker in a hospital setting. My role was to work with pregnant teenage girls, help disabled children and their families, and do child protection work in the hospital setting. Around this time, I also found out that Ambi had moved to Nottingham as her husband had a new job there; I thought that God had given me a chance to find her again. I made attempts to reconnect with her but it was clear she was not interested. Then, a few weeks later, I discovered that my first niece – Noor's daughter, who I had looked after and played with when she was a child – had got married. Even though Ambi had kept this from me, after the wedding was over, she called me to say that she had some clothes for me – a gift from Noor, this being the traditional practice in Sikh family weddings. My heart leapt: I saw this as a hand extended from Noor, and so Ambi and I arranged to meet. When we did, Ambi seemed very angry for some reason and I was upset, crying because I had not been told earlier about my first niece's wedding. As I reached out to take the suit she was offering, she suddenly snatched it away and stuffed it back in the bag. I had barely touched it and couldn't understand what she was doing. I had not been angry, just tearful. I had not said anything that would cause any disagreement, just expressed great sadness as I loved my niece dearly. She shook her head at me and walked off and I wondered if she was planning to take it back to Noor and say that I had refused to take it. I realised that in cultural and traditional terms, this would be such an insult to Noor, seen as a rejection of your relationship with your sister. Ambi clearly felt that I had no right to that relationship as a disowned woman. Any hope I had of reuniting with Noor felt like it had been taken away in that one action, by Ambi, who knew I would have no access to the others because of their husbands. She could have helped to unite us all again, but she chose not to. It occurred to me that Ambi was looking at a way to end all association with me.

I had other worries on my mind. It had been two years since my ectopic pregnancy and I still had not fallen pregnant. Philip and I were worried that I might not be able to conceive, as we had been told that this might happen, and we were both conscious of the fact that this could be the end of our family lines. Philip had no other siblings and his mother was also a single child. We decided that I should make an appointment at the fertility clinic. The consultant at the hospital sent me for a scan and there I had the biggest surprise of my life as I saw on the scanner screen a tiny life inside me. My joy at telling Philip and his ecstatic response was a turning point in our lives. I felt that God was giving us a chance, a reason to continue despite all that we had both been through.

Classically, I assumed that sickness in the first few months of pregnancy was normal, but it continued for the whole nine months. In the last few weeks, because I was so small and my stomach so big, I could hardly walk from one end of the room to the other. My size also meant that the obstetrician thought I should have an elective caesarean. Still, I was determined to turn things around and move on from the tragedy of the past and this event was so incredibly exciting. For the first time there was hope for us. Adam was born in March and we were probably the happiest parents ever! So we liked to believe. He was a big baby, 8lb 1oz, which was quite something for my tiny frame. He was beautiful and I felt I would burst with joy. Elizabeth and Edward came to see me at the hospital with flowers, as did friends from work, and when Philip brought us home and I walked into the house, there were vases full of daffodils in every corner of the living room. The sun shone and on that crisp afternoon, as Philip held Adam in his arms, I felt that my happiness was complete. Now this tiny person needed me, and I was going to be there for him 110%.

Shortly afterwards, to my great surprise and delight, my brother brought Mamaji to see me. It turned out that Ambi had told her I was expecting. She brought the traditional gift of a gold bangle for Adam. I helped her to hold him in her frail arms. In her advancing years, she was holding new life. She held him and her joy was clear to see. For those few hours, I wanted to believe that nothing could go wrong and that anything was possible. Philip looked concerned, knowing the hide-and-seek games that we had seen played out by my family before and worried about what would happen next but he was happy for me – my mother was holding my child! I was still hopeful, this time for my children. I didn't want them to be disowned like me. But I also knew that we would be kept hidden from the wider extended family and most likely not be seen by my siblings or mother for very long. As my brother left our house with my mother and his wife, I felt a mixture of hope and the accustomed feeling of being vulnerable.

I was determined to be a good mother however, and we did our best to be all the family Adam needed. There was just me, Philip, Adam and Philip's mum, who lived in another town. We felt the lack of family sharply at times, perhaps me more than Philip, who was used to being a single child. I recalled the large family of seven that I came from, and the extended family who would always be coming and going from the house, or us to theirs, joining together at weddings and celebrations at the Sikh temple.

Three years later, we had our daughter, Ami. She too was a gorgeous and much-wanted baby. She was also born by elective caesarean and after having her I was told that it would not be a good idea to have any more children because I now had a third scar, after my ectopic and then the birth of my son. We were happy with our two; I gave thanks to God for the many blessings in my life. I looked at this child in my arms as she slept, a much wanted little girl, a great joy for me, and I vowed that she would be loved unconditionally. We decided that Adam and Ami were 'Children of Hope'. A hope where life choices were not made for them, but support given for the good ones they made.

My mother visited again after Ami was born; she brought a gold bracelet for her granddaughter and held her with such pleasure. I knew that my two would probably be the last of her grandchildren: Ami was the tenth. I was sure that my parents would have lavished attention on them and would have seen them regularly but this too would have been kept secret from the others and my heart was heavy knowing that her other grandchildren would never be told of Adam and Ami's names or where they lived.

Philip, my children and I would never be part of the lives of this extended family. Such thoughts broke my heart.

During the months after the children were born, I would think of nothing else but my sisters, hoping that somehow they would care at this time, would ask to see the children, would see the connection with their lives and the lives of their own children. I was sure that my mother and Ambi had let Noor and Jay and their own children know about the birth; if they had not, it would only be time before they did. The lines of informing one normally does within families was blurred, if not distinctly missing, no communication, no shared joy and no compassion, a deafening silence leaving me confused and ultimately feeling punished. I shed the same silent tears that I shed at my father's funeral many a time and could not understand that such cruelty was possible. Despite this, I remained incredibly strong for my children, determined not to fail but to give them the best of myself. My determination was now even greater than any previous conviction, to not give in to the abuse that I had faced within the family.

I tried to come to terms with the situation with my sisters. Noor and I never connected again after she left for her marriage at seventeen – she had been like a mother to me, albeit only in practical ways, until that time. There had been several occasions when she could have reached out to me but I felt that she was not emotionally able to do that, due to her family's disapproval of me, my choice of independence and the hurt that this would have caused my parents. Once I was at a wedding with Philip and Adam, who was about a year old at this time. I was surprised that we had been asked – my brother's wife's sister was getting married and they wanted us to meet the girls' mother. I hadn't really wanted to go for fear of people's reaction, but on the other hand, wondered if this was at last a chance to get to know the members of my brother's wife's clan; they seemed to be more relaxed about my situation than my own family. Before the ceremony, we were standing in the dining room when Noor and Jay walked past us, avoiding eye contact; they said nothing. It took me by complete surprise – a possible fleeting moment of hope dashed so quickly, heartlessly, as if we were strangers passing each other on the street. Then I realised that Dev was also spurning us – he would not come near us and I knew that he was worried that people would stop talking to him if he didn't uphold the family honour. It was a painful experience, although I felt angry not for myself and Philip but for my son, the innocent child we held in our arms, that they could dismiss him in this way: it was such an act of cowardice and cruelty. He was young enough not to know, but I felt the pain for him. I watched my brother from the other side of the room and had to admit that I felt sorry for him: he had plenty of problems in his own life. Philip and I decided to go home before the marriage took place, and as we left, Dev followed us into the car park. He didn't push us to stay and I felt that he didn't know what to say or do, maybe ashamed of having put us in this dilemma in the first place. We said goodbye but Philip and I agreed on the way back that it was a mistake to have gone and that we did not want to expose our child to that kind of situation again. I wondered if I would ever be able to make Adam understand the reasons why my sisters had ignored him.

On another occasion, Noor and her husband were downstairs at my mother's house on a rare visit while my husband, my son and I were hidden upstairs. We had managed to arrange a visit when only my mother and brother were there, and Noor's arrival had not been expected. Dev told us to go upstairs and hide and we stayed there for what seemed like hours. We could hear laughter and noise and I held my son tight with tears streaming down my face until they had gone and it was safe for us to come down. Then Dev said he'd told them we were there. That was all too much for me. She could have asked to see us, or at least her nephew. These were the only times I got anywhere near my sisters. I would never have dared go to their homes as they had indeed made it clear that they could not bear to look at me....Jay and Ambi making this explicit, to keep away.

As for Ambi, I saw her briefly in 1989 when our sons were four months and seven months old respectively. She had a daughter, who was seven. I had never been allowed to be close to my niece so had barely got to know her, but I loved her from the brief episodes of contact we had. Ambi and I had seen each other occasionally before that — we were pregnant at the same time and I went to visit her two or three times but she was nervous in case her husband came home while I was there; on one occasion she was quite cruel and said that she needed to get on and I had to go. Her husband went to sit in the corner of the room with a newspaper in front of his face so that he would not have to communicate with me whilst I was there; my attempts at a respectful dialogue had no response. She came to see me after Adam was born but then I didn't hear from her for months. I eventually phoned her, worried that she would not be pleased to hear from me.

"Ambi, you've not phoned for ages," I said. "Is everything alright? I've left it for as long as I can to see if you would call…."

Her answer still echoes in my mind.

"What do you want with me?" she shouted. "I have a husband and two children to think of. Don't contact me again!" Then she hung up. I knew then that the door had not just been slammed shut, it had been locked. I never thought that Ambi would cut me out of her life so completely, but she did. I missed her terribly, but respected her wishes until four years later when I had to call her about a practical matter concerning our mother and she just hung up on me again. What point was there in trying any more?

I continued to have some minimal contact with my mother, although she had to keep this hidden from the rest of the family. I wished that my children could develop a connection with her and believed they had a right to know this side of the family, but she never warmed to us. I longed for some words of wisdom from her when I felt lost and confused but I still made excuses for her lack of communication, blaming her ill health for this as I had always done and feeling guilty for putting her in this situation. A year or so after Ami was born, I made one of my infrequent phone calls to her but on this particular occasion my brother's wife answered. She kept the conversation to a minimum, not knowing how much to share with this shunned woman, but explained that my mother had been taken to hospital. I was told that she had been in respite care as she was ill, so she was no longer living with my brother in the family home. I was shocked and upset; I had no idea how long Mamaji had been away from the family home and felt concerned for her. I was used to not being told about things that were going on in the wider family – births, marriages and deaths – and knew I was not considered worthy enough to be kept informed, but this was different. I was terrified that something serious might happen to my mother and they would not tell me because I clearly did not deserve to know. I felt so frustrated and helpless. When Philip came home from work, he found me in turmoil. As always, he comforted me and said that he would do whatever I felt was needed; he would support me if I wanted to go and see my mother. Despite the fact that she had never fought for me or stood by me, despite her rejection of me, my husband and children, despite everything, I still loved her, and believed that deep down, as a mother, she must love me and would want to see me.

"I want to go and see her, Philip," I said. We planned the visit with much thought and talk, then got in the car and drove to the hospital. When we arrived, I asked the nurses where we could find my mother, Mrs. Kaur. I explained that I was her daughter and had come from Nottingham; they seemed confused and suspicious, as if they didn't know anything about me. Of course, I would not have been mentioned by the family; I should have been used to this by now. We eventually found Mamaji sitting up in bed looking frail and it took her a few seconds to recognise me – the illness had worn her down. But it wasn't just the illness which had caused the lines on her face and the sadness in her eyes – my mother had had a hard life. She put on her glasses and looked nervous when she saw us, but asked about the children and we explained that they were at nursery. She said hello to Philip who was lovely as always, putting his hands together and saying, "Sat Sri Akal" (the traditional Sikh greeting); she returned the gesture with a weak smile. Then she looked around, at the corridor and the nurses' station, a worried expression on her face. I knew she was concerned that the family might turn up to visit at any moment and see us together. The idea of Philip and I – a 'mixed couple' – being seen in public with my mother would have been even worse than just seeing me on my own.

"You must go now," she said. Something in her voice made it sound so final, as though she was saying goodbye to me forever. I knew that I had to do the right thing by her; she was in hospital, unwell, what right had I to ask her to see me? I did not have the status required of a daughter any longer and I knew how angry her daughters and sons-in-law would be if they saw us. I was just glad to have seen her. Then, as I turned to go, she touched my arm.

"It's not your fault," she whispered. "It is your siblings who are at fault." I was amazed, and guessed that she knew about them all and especially how Ambi had shunned me, despite us both living in the same town. She said nothing more than that, and we had to do what she said and leave, even though it broke my heart. We drove back home in silence and I cried as we journeyed, realising that with those words my mother had dismissed me for the last time. I would never be able to contact her again, maybe never see her again. I could only guess at the impact these events would have in the years ahead; on me, Philip, and God forbid, my children. None of them deserved this treatment. I retreated into myself where it was easier for me to manage the sadness which was palpable and real. I could control my anger in this way. I was lost somewhere, where even Philip could not find me.

Chapter 9

I Won't Dance, Don't Ask Me

"I won't dance, don't ask me / I won't dance, don't ask me / won't dance, Madame, with you / My heart won't let my feet do things that they should do..."

(Dorothy Fields, Oscar Hammerstein II, Otto Harbach and Jimmy McHugh)

I n the end, the only thing for me to do was get on with my life and do the best I could for my own family – Philip, Adam and Ami. We moved home when Ami was three to start both children in independent schools; we wanted to give them a better chance not only in education but also in knowing their own self worth. It was a hard choice to make for many reasons, not least financially. We moved home twice, although we stayed in Nottingham. Philip and I worked hard to afford the life we had chosen, raising the children to the best of our abilities and finding an alternative to family within the Church and local community. During this time, my values were challenged and affirmed in various ways. Culturally and as an individual, I was learning that Britain was fast becoming a diverse society; as a family, we would go on to meet many people from different backgrounds and learn from their cultures. We thought ourselves fortunate to be able to delve into and experience other's backgrounds and also for our children to experience such a wide range of expression. They learnt African drumming and we sang together as a family in Gospel and Blues choirs, and met many dual heritage families. We realised that, to our advantage, our choices were not restricted by our parents or families so we could investigate and be part of many schools of learning.

When he was little, Adam made a friend at nursery who was an interesting boy, very sensitive, with an intuitive understanding of 'inclusion' and different cultures. He was from Iranian/white American background. We often met his mother when we went to collect Adam and she would chat with us. We became friends with her and her family, and the two children played together at each other's houses. Ami was a baby at this time. We learnt that they were members of the Baha'i faith. The Baha'is' believe in God and describe their faith as an independent world religion, although they accept the validity of most major religions; the central idea of the faith is unity and they believe that people should work together for the common benefit of humanity. We were invited to attend some of their events, and there we discovered that they had values and virtues from all the major religions of the world. Many of the Baha'is we met were mixed-race couples themselves and they were positive about multi-cultural relationships. Seeing so many mixed-race parents with their children also gave Philip and me the affirmation that despite my family's prejudice towards us as a mixed couple, there were many good examples of such relationships in this diverse and vibrant community.

Philip and I felt accepted and supported in their gatherings, and they actively promoted our own cultures, wanting to share food and information about our backgrounds. This was also very constructive for our children, who attended their Sunday school with other mixed-race children and adults alike. I knew from my reading and research as a social worker that children of mixed heritage needed positive role models and affirmation of their identity, and given that none of my family were around to provide this natural sense of who they were and where they belonged, we realised that linking with the Baha'is would be a great support for us in raising our children. Members of the group were very encouraging and loving towards Adam and Ami, who gained the appreciation that friends can be 'family' as much as (or even more than) birth-related people. They also learnt that they did not need to feel different from anyone else, even though they lacked the extended families that others enjoyed. They became independent very early on as a result with little restriction on their own creativity and decisions, not so much streetwise as mixing with safe people and doing safe things, as this was what was ingrained in them from the adults and families that cared for them. They also learnt to network and plan their social calendars from a very young age! I think they appreciated this and it helped them feel positive about their mixed identity: they were, as the Baha'is believed, the 'Flowers of One Garden'. But deep down, Philip and I felt that our faith was not truly Baha'i, even though we were told that our actions and input made us good Baha'is. We decided to carry on attending Church, raising our children as the Christians that Philip and I already were, all of us getting involved musically and in worship.

Then, in 2003, there was a review in my department at the Council and after nearly sixteen years in hospital social work, I requested a move to a different department which dealt with fostering and adoption. I was interested in that kind of work and felt I had the skills and experience to do it. I had to apply and be interviewed, but got the post along with some long-term colleagues with whom I had always enjoyed a good relationship. My duties included supporting foster carers and adopters who had children placed with them, and during this time I came across young Asian women who had become pregnant outside marriage without the knowledge of their families. They hid their pregnancy for as long as they could, sometimes until the baby was ready to be born, and then they would relinquish the child to the local authority, not knowing what else to do. Because of my own experiences, I understood their plight and knew the difficulties they were facing from their families with their traditional attitudes to shame and honour.

These were the things I put my energy into, and for the next few years we fully enjoyed our children's development and valued our time with them. But being a parent is not easy without the framework of support that exists in an extended family; sometimes I think that being a parent in such an isolated family was harder than I was prepared to admit but I was determined to succeed: if I failed, where would we go? As a social worker I had learnt that no family is perfect and it really is up to each of us to find ways of succeeding and meeting our children's needs.

What I also learnt from this time was how important it is for people like me who have been rejected by their families to be able to find a sense of community, even if it is not with our own kin. I realised how difficult and confusing it can be to find your place in a completely different society with different rules and values, especially if you come from a sheltered background as I had originally. But there is a need in us all for social contact; it is like a vacuum that has to be filled, and finding like-minded groups of people who accept you for who you are and don't judge that can make a great difference to the quality of your life. That need in us is a legacy from our parents, who raised us based on their own experiences of being raised; I grew up in a very large traditional family with strong religious values and a defined culture. I initially found it particularly difficult to be on my own, or just with Philip and the children, as I had no access to the things that had once been the framework of my life – attending family gatherings, celebrating the many achievements of my relatives, especially my nieces and nephews, and marking important events such as funerals (I was forever worrying about who might have died, knowing that I would not be told). I missed the festivals that happened in the wider Sikh community and the weddings, which would draw everyone in the clan together for eating, laughing and sharing humour. We would make chapattis together at the temple, talk to the bride and her sisters and the other women who were invited to help with the wedding festivities that went on. These were the things that gave meaning to our lives and they all revolved around people socialising; the lack of this left a huge gap in my life. I know I experienced sad and difficult times growing up, and that my family had their difficulties with communication, but I did experience many good things – I appreciated many aspects of my cultural background, young people like me within the Sikh community that shared the same jokes and sense of humour, the Sikh religion, with its many good values, and understood the importance of the family's social events. Despite the faults many of us found with them as we grew up – as in any community – they always managed to find the good things that would get them through their often difficult times. However, I experienced most of this as a child, not as an adult, and I am not sure how it would have been for me if I had done what was expected of me and stayed, married a man of my parents' choosing, served my in-laws and given up my chance at a career. I made the choice not to find out because of the difficult things that I saw the adults in my family and clan experiencing. For now, I had to do the right thing for my children and Philip, so I put the need for peace in my life in God's hands. Deep down, though, I missed the family terribly and continued to love them. At times the stark void of them not wanting to know me was very frightening; I wondered if my siblings or my mother thought about me. Did they think they could have coped with such a lonely situation? Never a day went by when I didn't think of them all, and during my children's teens, time and time again I would go over in my mind how I could approach my mother and my siblings.

I did not have any further contact with my mother after that day in 1993 when we went to see her in hospital in Birmingham. It had been my one last chance at trying to find out if she wanted to know me, see me, but she didn't. I had been right to believe that she had cut me out of her life. That goodbye was what she wanted, she told me that loud and clear. What can you do when your own mother tells you to go? Says she does not want to see you again? What is there left to say? Yet again I consoled myself that this was my mother's life and her world was a different world, that she could not help this, and that her other daughters and their husbands were her life now; she was prepared to forgo the relationship with me for that. I was not angry with her for thinking this, I did not challenge it. I knew she was an ill woman and you cannot argue with or confront someone who has been through so much and seen so much pain. Then again, I also knew she would say that there was nothing else she could do; I had heard her say this enough times. I felt the pain for my own children more than anything. How do you tell your children that their grandmother chooses not to know them? To this day, I question whether it was because of the family that she did not want to see me and the children, or if she simply had no love to give. Did she know how to love? How was she able to give up on my children so easily? How was that possible? Did she suffer so much with her health that there was no more she could deal with? She was quite possibly unable to empathise with me, as her world had been so different from mine. She did not know how to treat me, as the way I behaved did not fit the culture of her time. Sometimes I wondered if she thought that because I had managed to survive independently – in a way a woman in my situation could never survive in India – I should be happy with my life and go and live it and enjoy it, knowing that the others would never accept this, and that the price we had to pay was permanent estrangement.

My brother chose not to keep in touch either, and I had long ago given up on my sisters. It was very hard not to give in and crumble and I had to find ways of coping. Philip was always steadfast and believed in me and helped by listening; I also always felt that someone was looking over me, despite everything. I was provided for, loved by Philip, had the most beautiful children, and was able to get out of bed each morning and get on with the routine and structure of my day doing a job I enjoyed. I wanted to develop as a person so that I was better able to give to others; I knew I had a lot to learn, having realised early on that my upbringing had been very sheltered and I often got things wrong (in fact, probably still do!), and it was only at school that I found role models to which I could aspire. I realised that I had to learn many things by taking small steps, and that this would take a long time.

After many years of silence from my family, we were happy and settled in our home; Philip and I were still working hard at our careers and the children, now sixteen and thirteen, were doing well at school. That year, we decided to take a weekend break without the children and planned a drive across the country to the West Midlands with stays in hotels en route. By chance we found ourselves in the area where my family home was and where my brother used to live. On impulse, I asked Philip to drive to his house. Before I had time to think about what I was doing or how my brother might react, or even if he would still be there, I found myself knocking on his front door. Philip was saying, "Are you sure you want to do this?" when the door opened and there was Dev. He had aged considerably. Before I could open my mouth to speak, he fell to the floor in the hallway as if in shock. I didn't know what to think and could hardly make out what he was saying, so I bent down and then realised what he was telling me.

"It's our mother," he said. "Mamaji is dead. She died four years ago."

I could not believe what I was hearing. Suddenly his wife appeared; she comforted him and tried to help him up. He sat there as if in a daze and began to talk rapidly, saying that he had not known how to reach me to tell me, that he had thought of hiring a private detective to find me to tell me of our mother's death, though for some reason had not. As I listened to his excuses, I knew that he would have told everyone in the family the same thing, and not being able to find me would prove that I was a runaway (which was marginally less shameful to the family than being disowned). I looked at his face to see if there was any truth in what he was saying or any trace of guilt, but it was hard to tell. I wondered if it was some kind of act, designed to cover his guilt at not having told me before. I could not bear to hear any more and needed to get away to come to terms with what I had just heard but managed to keep my composure as we were leaving, not showing any indication to him of my feelings. I still worried that he could be the only link in the family willing to see the children and provide some answers for them, and the changes in my family's life over the last thirty two years. Dev agreed that we could come back the next day and talk.

I did not cry, but that evening when we sat down to eat the special meal that had been prepared for us at the hotel, I could not touch my food. I did not know what to feel, and that surprised me, but I realised that this news of my mother's death was going to take its toll on me and I would need time to take it in. Over the years, I had built up a level of protection inside, knowing that when she died I might not be informed; I was half expecting this after Dev only told me begrudgingly about my father's death several days after the event. I did not sleep all night, tossing and turning, and by the next morning I realised that I was in shock and unable to absorb or process things.

"Am I so bad that they couldn't share that news with me?" I cried while Philip held me in his arms. "Why would someone not tell their sibling about the death of their mother?"

At that moment, I felt so cut off from my family that I might as well have been dead myself, and I knew that I would never be informed of the deaths of my siblings either. As arranged, we went back to Dev's house where we sat numbly while he told us that Mamaji had died peacefully in her sleep at a nursing home. I asked if she had mentioned me or the children before she died but he said no, she had not. He told us very little about her last few years of life, although I was not surprised by this, as silence had often been used by my family as a way of controlling others and covering up guilt. In the end we said our goodbyes, offering half-hearted promises to keep in touch. Dev expressed an interest in meeting Adam and Ami but I did not feel it was the right time – Adam was halfway through his GCSEs and I thought it would be too disruptive; I said I would contact him to arrange a meeting at a later date. Just before we left, Dev pulled a business card out of his pocket which had Philip's number on it – I couldn't believe my eyes but said nothing about his earlier lies about not being able to contact me. What was the point?

After my return to home, I had no one apart from Philip and my children to talk to. We told them of their grandmother's death, but I protected them from the harshness of the truth and how these circumstances had affected me. They were old enough to ask questions and I wanted to be able to answer them honestly. I had tried to raise the topic of my family to enable them to understand their roots, and now I was ready to answer those deeper questions as and when they wanted to know. It took me some weeks to sort my head out and realise that I would never get answers to questions about my mother's death and her life in all those years that I had not seen her, or how things were for her in the Asian nursing home, run by a friend of Jay's who had seemed distant and been unkind to me at my father's funeral. In the end I decided to bring it up with my team manager at work, as it must have been obvious that I was upset. She listened and offered to put a referral in for me to have counselling with Relate. I found this helpful as I didn't know who else to turn to. It was very painful going through this and as the appointments were during my lunch hour, returning to work in the afternoon was always hard. I still felt incredibly alone, and going back through my early life and later experiences with the counsellor somehow made me feel the loneliness even more strongly. Also, I was not used to sharing these feelings with anyone, partly because I needed the help to express them and make sense of them. However, I realised that this was important for me. She told me that I was not angry and that I needed to be angry, and I recall thinking that I was too frightened to be angry; what would it achieve? There were very few people I could talk to about the anger I felt without them saying that it was better to forget it and move on, because they did not know what else to say. It was like a private tragedy that could not be shared casually with just anyone. How do you explain the fact that you only just found out that your mother died four years ago and that you had not seen her for at least eight years before that? It was hard for people to appreciate the enormity of this and the long-term effects it had. The counsellor from Relate was very good and she even shared tears with me towards the end. This was for me a true counsellor who listened and felt how I was feeling. She helped me to get it all out for the first time and I started to write things down, as I found that I could express my feelings, especially the anger, more easily that way. I also tried to remember some of the good things about my mother, her smile, her joy at seeing the children when she did, her small gifts to me. I tried to remember more – her cooking, what she had told me about her life as a child, her life with her parents, her blind mother and how that must have been for her. I struggled to recall what she had told me about what she wanted to do, like going to school, and wondered what it had been like for her being married to my father and the years she had been without him, both when he sent her back to India alone and after he died.

I suppose I could have refused to talk to my brother again after the incident at his house but I tried to be wise and think of my children and the fact that Dev was their uncle and the only member of my family with whom we had any contact. We did try to arrange to meet up again but something always seemed to get in the way and Dev was never exactly keen to keep in touch. I made another attempt at reconciliation with him after the children started asking questions about the family. They were teenagers and curious about their relatives and wanted to meet their mother's brother. Dev may not have wanted a relationship with me and my family and we all knew that he risked being ostracised by the wider family if they learnt of his association with me; still, we decided to talk to him and his wife again. It was perhaps my only chance of giving the children a link to their extended family and answers to their questions. This would also be someone that their mother grew up with, someone who they could call Uncle. After much careful consideration, planning and thought with regard to our children's possible reaction we arranged to go to Pizza Hut one afternoon all together. Adam and Ami were quiet at first but then they opened up and were soon sharing jokes and even laughed about our likeness. It went as well as it could have under the circumstances, and we agreed to see each other again.

I admit that I was nervous about these meetings, mainly because I feared that this contact could be cut off at any minute; that my children would find themselves confused and lost, just as I had been. It was a lonely place and I didn't want them to end up there. Still, I remained calm and hopeful that this relationship might be promising for them. Dev and I were in our mid-forties by then, and I hoped that life had taught us what was important and that the next generation need not have to deal with the problems of the previous one. My job in Social Services had taught me that contact with the family is very important for children; mine did not know my brother well but they knew that he was their uncle and that this was their only chance to get to know one of their relatives on their mother's side. In the September of 2005, some months after Dev told me about our mother's death, it was Philip's fiftieth birthday and we decided to invite Dev and his wife to the celebrations which we had organised. Dev was actually keen to come and although I knew I had to be realistic and did not want my children hurt if things didn't turn out well, I hoped that this could be the start of a new chapter in our lives.

After this party for Philip, we had hopes for the children that their uncle would keep in touch. I was pleased that they had seen my brother again; he could see how well they had done and what lovely young people they were.

As the weeks went on, we heard nothing from Dev or his wife. I phoned to speak with him twice and his wife would keep me on the phone, but say that he was not home. I thought it strange, so I tried calling another time when I knew he should definitely be home. This time, he answered and we spoke. After a while, I realised that our families' relationship was not meant to be. He was not able to be honest about his intentions, which appeared half-hearted, or about his commitment towards seeing us. I could not understand why he had decided to reject us again, just when I thought we had put our differences behind us, but he said it was too difficult. I had to accept that this brief contact with him had broken down, and I was so upset for the children.

Philip and I felt we had to do something after this conversation with Dev and in the end I asked Philip to speak to him, using the phone in the bedroom while I sat at the top of the stairs. I didn't want either of them to hear me crying and thought it would be better if Philip could talk to Dev 'man to man'.

"Simran is distraught about why you don't want to keep in touch," I heard him say. "Why have you not kept in touch?"

Philip's voice was usually peppered with humour so it was strange to hear him sounding so serious and standing up for our small family. He was quiet as he listened to what Dev had to say and at the end, his voice was calm. "So just to be absolutely clear," he said, "you are saying that you are making the choice to have no contact with us?" My heart went out to Philip then. I knew he had understood how important it was for me to know that I had done everything I could to keep the relationship with Dev, that I would always have been in a quandary if I thought I could have done more. Even then, Philip was careful not to appear to be cutting the link with Dev, saying that the 'ball was in his court'. He asked Dev to stay on the line a little longer, to see if there was any way for us to find a way forwards, to clarify where we were again, but Dev put the phone down. We would not hear from Dev again.

After the phone call we talked, Philip clearly affected and angry for the way that I had been treated, how we all as a family had been treated. He had never expressed very much in the years leading to this, always the supporter, always taking my lead. He had suffered too, tried to make sense of it, knowing that families all over the world have difficulties and disagreements which it takes hard work to overcome. In my family, he had met a very hard wall; we were always vulnerable to failure and it had been a constant battle. We had always been on a thin line with my family and here was Dev saying he did not want to know.

Philip eventually explained that my brother was more concerned about keeping relations with my sisters and their families than with us, as keeping contact with us was "too difficult". And yet Dev also told him that he had thought of coming to our city to have my sister Ambi tie a 'Rahki' (sacred thread) around his wrist to celebrate 'Raksha Bandhan', a festival which recognises the relationship between brothers and sisters. The tying of the thread symbolises the sister's love and prayers for her brother's well-being and the brother's lifelong vow to protect her. It was very painful for me, as a sister, not to be included in that.

I felt deep down that Dev had done his best. I realised how hard it had been for him to admit that he was in touch with us, but wished that he could see how painful it was for my children to be rejected for reasons that made no sense to them – we were family after all. I often thought of my own nieces and nephews; I knew that they would only have heard the worst said by their parents about us. I had to stop grieving about this, but felt the injustice of it all. My thoughts about them were very deep, and I would have done anything to see them. I counted them all and would berate myself when I started to forget names and birthdays and did not know who had married who or which children I was Great Auntie to. I spent hours working out how old everyone was and then wondering if I had the dates wrong. These were the feelings that all came back when I thought about that final contact with Dev, but to be honest I had no choice but to shut them out and get on with day to day living. Then one day in 2006, after months of grieving this situation with Dev, an event occurred that changed many things from then on.

Chapter 10

Lifelines

"But those who hope in the Lord will renew their strength. They will soar on wings like eagles; they will run and not grow weary, they will walk and not be faint."

(Isaiah 40:31)

I have worked since I was seventeen and have always thrown myself into it wholeheartedly. Work gave me consistency, stability and routine and a purpose for daily life. I recognised this in others who had been in similar situations to mine, the 'survivors', as we called ourselves, who I started to meet around 2006. The events leading up to meeting these men and women ultimately gave me strength to search for my recovery, and the hope that what I found might help others find the same.

For some years, Philip and I had given everything to the children, trying to protect them from the circumstances that I faced because of my family. I had managed to contain my feelings as long as I could, mainly because I wanted to prove that I could do this, but deep down things were obviously not going so well and sometimes I felt very low. These were also the teenage parenting years and I was being tested as a mother: that was a tall order for me in itself. Everything in my mind was ruled by the loss that I experienced in my family and the lack of healing from my past. One day everything came to a head; for some reason all the feelings I had shut away for all those years came flooding back and I could no longer contain them. I came home from work and, when I went to my bedroom to change into something more comfortable, I began to cry and couldn't stop. I didn't know what to do with myself. I had no clue where to run to and worse, had no one to unburden myself to. I was in the dangerous waters of 'not talking', as I was so accustomed to my family doing. Philip and I shared the parenting and all that it involved but at that moment I felt I had no more to give to life or our relationship. I don't know where this came from or why. My job was difficult at times but I had always prided myself on what I could do and what I might achieve. Yet now I did not feel that I had control over my life any more. I don't know how long I was there for, crumpled in a heap on the floor, but I was eventually found by Philip who crouched down beside me and tried to comfort me. I cried aloud – something I would never normally do; usually I'd be screaming inside, unable to get the words out. I cried that I was not worthy, that I had no reason to exist: this was what my family had told me and I should accept what they wanted, which was for me to disappear. I was dead to them and therefore I should be dead to the rest of the world. It made complete sense to me at that moment: the family that I had been born into did not know whether I was alive or dead and they did not care. Our upbringing, morals, values, identity and self-worth all come from our families and as I did not have this from mine, it seemed pointless to carry on. I had nothing to give. Philip was very concerned, telling me that this was not true. His eyes were wet with tears too: despite his incredible support, here I was years down the line still trying to cope away from the family of my birth, still struggling with their values that were supposed to be my values too. It was as if I was tired of trying to rise above my family's lack of belief in me, and felt that I could no longer do it alone.

That night I spoke with my friend Satinder on the phone. She had been a team manager in one of my posts in social work and we had kept in touch. We had often talked about parenting and I would turn to her for support in the absence of anyone else that I could go to for this. She suggested that I should go and see my GP. Initially I was reluctant to take her advice as ironically, being a professional myself, I had always fought against consulting a professional and did not think that seeing a doctor would help. I did not consider myself ill, just stuck with the experiences that still lurked deep within me, and certain that what had happened to me could not be understood by anyone, especially not by people from outside my culture. The counselling sessions that I had with Relate helped but they had clearly not been enough. Most people didn't know how to react to my disownment, either because they did not understand, or they misjudged the reasons why. They would make judgements without realising exactly what the situation was and never seemed comfortable asking questions, so as to not offend, for instance. So I protected myself. Social work could be a very judgemental field, depending on what you were dealing with. I realise now that the concept of honour and shame from my background were far removed from the lives of many of the people around me: it must have seemed unbelievable that honour-based issues could remove a person from their family and community. My friend persuaded me I needed to talk to someone about how the impact of these events was affecting my life. I therefore, reluctantly but out of desperation, made an appointment with a GP for the following day.

My GP, Dr Lott, was, and still is, a godsend. The first time I saw her, I cried so much she couldn't understand what I was saying. I was put on Prozac and told to come back in a few days; she listened week after week while I cried. This helped, allowing me to grieve and make sense of the process of what I called my 'breakdown'. Dr Lott being there for me has undoubtedly helped in the process of my recovery. I explored further help with her, and was referred for psychotherapy. It was interesting to discover that under the Health Service, there is little help for cases like mine where family breakdown has occurred and recovery is a struggle. These issues are not considered a priority of any sort, and this made me think of the many men and women that I had met who were at an earlier stage of the recovery process. Where would they get their help from? What chance had they got? I was grateful that I had a good GP who was willing to try to understand my situation. It took some time, due to waiting lists under the Health Service, but I was eventually referred to a student psychotherapist who happened to be Asian.

"Why didn't you seek help before?" she asked. This was the most poignant question asked of me during this period.

My answer was simple enough: "I never thought anyone would listen to my story; I didn't think anyone would believe me or could understand what being disowned was like."

It's an answer that I went on to hear many survivors of abuse and honour crimes give to professionals and friends alike.

Although I was able to talk through and understand more about my feelings with the therapist, it did not help as much as the individual counselling that I had received through Relate, or indeed Dr Lott. These two people had truly listened and raised questions that were appropriate for my situation, things that I had never spoken about in all the years I had carried around the hurt that my family had caused. The counsellor at Relate helped me to see that I had always subconsciously believed that the things that were done and said to me were 'normal' within the confines of my family, that I felt that I was the one who had been in the wrong, not them. I could not stand up to them or argue my case because they would morally justify their stance and make me feel worthless. Whenever I approached members of my family or came within their sight, their dismissal, rejection and unreasonable anger time after time made it very hard to know what I could or should do. This, coupled with my own vulnerability, fear of breaking down, of losing it altogether, made it almost impossible for me to explain this to people outside the world of these experiences.

It took time to work through what was happening to me, but the support given to me by Philip, his selfless commitment to me when I was at my most vulnerable and very low, gave me the strength to go on. Getting through the day was hard but Philip would always be there, not only for me but for our two hormonal teenagers as well. I felt guilty that I had brought this on Philip, but he reminded me that he had a choice and it was me he chose to be with. He loved me unconditionally. At times I felt as though I was wandering around in the dark, allowing myself for the first time to look at the devastation that I felt about our situation and only able to take so much of the 'normal' anger that teenagers display. We had no extended family to help us through these times, no respite from the confines of our small family where all had to be contained and managed by ourselves. I told my children that their grandparents would have loved them, that they would have been called by the affectionate Punjabi names that I had used since they were tiny. I never spoke badly of my family to my children, only telling them that they did not want to speak with me, trying to give an appropriate explanation, but never an untruth. As they got older I provided more information on their request, never avoiding their questions and curiosity. My son went through a period when he wanted to meet his cousins, but my daughter would say, "Well I've never known them so I don't know what I'm missing."

Sometimes anger would surface inside me at the cruel way that they had been rejected too, despite the fact that their existence was known to the clan through my mother and brother and the grapevine in the Sikh community. My family were able to hide from their responsibilities in another town, in a world where their community supported their choice to disown those who don't fit.

Although I was plunged into the depths of despair at times, I knew I had to surface somehow and keep my head above water for all our sakes. I was working in a stressful job but this had been my saving grace too, being able to have a routine and also making changes to peoples' lives where I was able to, supporting others who I could empathise with. Working with the children we looked after and their foster carers was something that I could relate to. These kids had parents who had rejected them or had not been able to care for them for whatever reason. I would look into their faces and see how much family meant to them. They wanted to be included and would seek attention as if to say, "Look at me! I'm not invisible! I am a human being." They needed to be treated like any 'normal' children, even if they couldn't be with their birth family like many others around them. I admired the foster carers who were able to give these children hope by showing that friends can be family too – something I have always believed is possible. Knowing how it was for looked-after children, I was never bitter or thought that I should have more than I had, and was happiest when plans for the children went well at work, seeing them bonding with their carers and receiving unconditional love, despite the challenges that this presented. Both carers and children taught me a lot: what neglect was, what was right and wrong, what abuse meant, what it meant to be powerless. I also saw families go through difficulties and empathised with their situations and despite trying to give their all, how hard it was for them, just like my family. I knew that there were children who would return home to their families and that as social workers we wanted this to work well for them. We tried to keep families together as much as we struggled to keep the children safe. I was under no illusion that things were easy for these families, but I learnt that it was possible to be loved by a 'substitute' family. Of course, I thought about this in the context of my own life and could not forget desperately trying to connect with my brother and Ambi, my mother and father – I still found it hard to grasp what it was that I had done that was so bad, so unforgivable, that I could not be accepted by my family. This situation did not necessarily mean that it impacted on my work – if anything, what it did was help me to focus on the change that was possible for children, to have hope, to look at ways not only to protect children, but to be able to empathise with their experience of loss. Also to support those caring for them to feel supported with their task of managing the various needs of the children as a result of their loss.

So many times I would tell Philip that I was going to knock on my siblings' doors and he would look concerned because of the rejection he knew I would face and the impact it would have on me each time. He had experienced my silences, and each time I tried and was rebuffed I would end up task-centred, on automatic pilot, doing no more than enough to get us through each day at home. He began to see a pattern where it could take months, sometimes years, for me to enjoy life to the full again. Once I realised this, I knew that I had to do something to turn this nightmare into something better and more sustainable in my life.

Initially I raised the knocking on the doors of my siblings with the counsellor. She did not want me to go there. I'd introduced this in the middle of my sessions with her and she made me think about how I would cope with the inevitable rejection. What consequences would it have on my health and how might it impact on Philip and the children? I then went through different possible solutions – I was convinced that there was something 'out there', some kind of agency, something like the post-adoption service we had in fostering and adoption, where men and women like me could have help in contacting our families, getting advice on how we could be united. The counsellor went away and tried to find such agencies but she couldn't find anything.

I would not believe the counsellor. I said, "Surely there must be somewhere in the UK where there is help for those who have been disowned and want to try to re-establish links with their families?"

I had clearly invented the idea in my mind but found it hard to believe that something like this did not exist in this day and age. The counsellor gave me the names of some places in London that do work with individuals on family situations, but they were costly services; I thought I could do better than that with the disowned Asian men and women that I had met, through sharing our common experiences.

More importantly, I began to ask myself *why not?* Why did the service not exist for disowned Asian men and women? I felt that there should be some sort of service that was needs-led and which put disowned people in touch with their families, a bridging or reconciliation service that was easily accessible to victims. I realised that the shame dynamic often meant that victims would find it enormously difficult to make an approach to their family because of the possibility of further rejection.

The help I had received after the breakdown meant that my relationship with Philip grew from this point. We were stronger and wiser than in the early years of our marriage, when we threw ourselves into being parents and lost ourselves in the day-to-day routines, supporting our children. We have not looked back since. It also made me more determined to try to find a way of enabling others to find the right help, to continue to fight not just for myself and the people I loved who were innocently caught up in the situation – my husband and children – but also for the many people out there that I had come to know, or knew of, who were struggling with the same issues. Over the years I had developed an interest in mixed relationships, especially where there was family and community opposition in them being together. Not all the couples I met had the same problems as me, I hasten to add, but it was good to know that I was not alone; there were marked similarities in many of our journeys where we had to deal with our families' rejection and disownment.

In November 2006, I bought myself a laptop and started searching on Google for anything I could find about disownment and mixed relationships. One day, I came across a website called MixTogether.org. It was started by a young man as the result of his experience as the white partner facing opposition from his Asian girlfriend's family. When I read what he said on his site about his and other's experiences, I felt a huge sense of relief, that there was someone out there who could actually acknowledge this issue with the truth of what it could be like for mixed Asian/white couples in these circumstances. There were not many posts up at that time as the site was very new, but I knew that at last I had found a place where I and others like me had a chance of being understood.

He had experienced the problems that couples of mixed race, colour and religion face growing up in a multicultural society as a white male, while I had experienced them as an Asian female. It was clear to him that children from different cultures were being taught about equality in school but it wasn't always being practiced at home. He also knew that there were success stories which should be told in order to give hope and encouragement to others who wanted to make their own choices. The problem was, he said, that there was no one place where all that experience and knowledge was shared and recorded in a searchable form. There was no forum where mixed couples could just meet up and chat to each other in order to find support and understanding. He decided to set up a website where problems could be aired, information shared and support given, no matter what the background or status of that person was.

I started to type in my story, tentatively at first, but I do remember being very tearful, and it was as if the floodgates had opened – I couldn't stop. Over the next few days, I received replies from the other members, telling me that they understood and opening up about their own lives and experiences. We carried on exchanging posts and as time went by, more and more people joined the forum. To my surprise, hundreds of people read my posts and many of them sent me personal messages; some said that they were shocked by the way I had been treated, others identified with the pain that I described and some were going through the same. At last I had faith and hope that there were others who might understand what it was like being in a mixed relationship where the issues of shame and honour were prevalent. This was being affirmed and acknowledged, and that was pretty amazing. Not only that, but the cultural and traditional aspects of disownment were being aired through the forum, which promised "support to couples where they face opposition from family or community". MixTogether became a lifeline I could hang on to.

It occurred to me that my family would be more likely to use the excuse of a mixed relationship to cast judgement on me now and explain their rejection of me, and yet the real issues were about me being 'different', for not having an arranged marriage, for leaving home, being independent and choosing my own destiny. I realised that the two – forced marriage and free choice – were entwined, linked, and greatly misunderstood. Ashley from MixTogether seemed touched by my story and commitment to the forum. He asked for my view about things and whether I would help to develop 'MT'.

The first time we met was when he asked me to attend a meeting he had arranged with the organisation Karma Nirvana. I knew about 'KN', as I had read a book called 'Shame' which was written by its co-founder, Jasvinder Sanghera (Philip and I bought the book on the first day it came out after my friend Baldeep in Australia recommended it to us and we read it avidly). In the book, Jasvinder tells her story: how she left home at a young age rather than accept a forced marriage and was disowned. Her sister committed suicide because of her own desperately unhappy forced marriage. In fact, I wrote to her after I read it; so much of her story echoed mine and I said that I had wanted to write about my experiences for many years and it felt like she had written some of that for me.

MixTogether wanted to form links with KN to expand on the work we were doing and was also going to help with their IT system. I was reluctant to go to the meeting at first and did not want to be exposed to Asian workers, a mistrust that developed from being rejected in the past. I didn't think I would be strong in those days with all the stress and unhappiness that I had gone through already. I am glad that I took the chance to go. I felt that it would be good to meet others like me and see how they had coped; I knew that Jasvinder had struggled alone with her problems for as long as I had. Jasvinder was not there at the first meeting but apparently my colleague from MixTogether had told her about me and my experiences; I went on to meet her at a training day for survivors where she asked for supporters to help her launch the 'Honour Network Helpline', a project designed to support victims and survivors of forced marriage and honour-based violence.

I stood up to volunteer and shared my story; surprisingly, I got a round of applause. There was such joy in meeting other survivors like myself at this event and as I went round and talked to everyone, we drank tea and ate jelabis which was something familiar that we could all relate to. Jasvinder said she was looking for survivors who were prepared to have their pictures shown on leaflets and to speak on platforms for the campaign against forced marriage and honour-based violence; she also wanted help with setting up and running the helpline.

I began working as a volunteer for KN. Jasvinder told me later that she was grateful to Ashley for introducing us; she acknowledged that she had received my letter but had not yet had chance to respond to it. A day was organised for a photo session of the team and some of the survivors which would be put on leaflets and posters and sent out to various organisations around the country. We highlighted the cases of the girls and women who didn't survive, who had been murdered because of 'forbidden' relationships which were sometimes from within their own community. The injustice of this would remain with me every time.

The campaign against forced marriage was very important and it was clear that many people needed safe refuges and practical help in rebuilding their lives; however, I also knew that there were men and women out there who wanted to choose their own partner and needed help in standing up for their relationships in the face of family and community opposition. The idea of campaigning for the rights of couples who wanted to make these choices was in my view far from the minds of a large part of our communities and I wanted that change. I realised that I got a great deal of strength from the help that I could give others in hope of better relationships with their families. I was always unhappy when I heard real-life stories of anger and the rejection of mixed relationships, many of them within the Asian community, the difference of caste or religion cited as 'justifiable reasons'. I met single people at Karma Nirvana who Jasvinder called survivors, with horrific stories of honour-based violence and rejection. I knew that family was very important to everyone, no matter where in the world, so my work on MT was focused on trying to help people keep communication open in the hope that families would not shut individuals out.

Ashley was present when the Honour Network Helpline was launched by KN. Survivors came on stage to give their stories of forced marriage and disownment. The conference was attended by every agency that I could think of: police officers of high standing, Asian professionals, social workers, teachers, counsellors, psychotherapists, doctors and judges, all present to hear our stories. Jasvinder asked me to take the stand to explain my story; she said that she had never met someone else who had been disowned for longer than herself and she called us all the 'honourable ones'. I was not nervous about telling my story, in fact I was ready and willing to speak, not just for myself but for many others, and was grateful to be able to talk about my experiences. It was the first time that I had stood up in public to tell the world about what happened to me with my family, what it was like to be disowned, never to receive a birthday card from family, nor celebrate Diwali or Christmas with them, not being able to sleep under the same roof as them or feel that you belong and share life with them. To have the next generation disowned too.

My colleague from MixTogether and Philip sat together at a table at this event; it meant a great deal to me that Jasvinder had invited them. I spoke about MixTogether and the support that I had received from them and the importance of the work that we were doing. We gave out many business cards that day for MT. I recall saying on stage that my parents had never forced me into a marriage but had rejected me for not taking the one they offered, for making my own choice and wanting independence and a better life than the one they were able to offer me. Many tears were shed, or kept just under the surface, by all of us through the day; it was an incredibly difficult thing to do but it was one of the most empowering days we had ever known. A sense of relief prevailed as we all hugged each other. We hoped that the agencies would understand the issues involved and that no matter what role they played, they would recognise that both 'cultural sensitivity' and 'political correctness' could cost lives.

I began to get stronger. The anti-depressants, counselling and psychology had enabled me to cope up to a point, but the people I linked with at MT and KN helped me to heal, gave me direction and inspired me to continue to fight. I enjoyed my increasing commitment to both groups and loved being able to give back some of the positive energy I was receiving, not just from MixTogether and Jasvinder but from Philip and the children too. Jasvinder and I spent some years in a close and connected relationship which I have valued immensely, and I learnt much from her. We connected through our faith in Jesus, and built the foundation for this friendship and our lives.

Also around this time I met Mervena, a foster carer at a support group I ran for the foster carers who had teenagers placed with them. Mervena had an amazing ability to befriend and include people. Her openness and kindness to others was obvious to see. She also taught me a lot about Christianity; she explained that Jesus' name in the Hebrew language of his time was 'Yeshua' and the Hebrew name for God is 'Yahweh'. I remembered that my mother would use these names which she must have learnt from the Christians she met in India. My interest in the real history of my faith was ignited from this meeting with my friend.

Mervena invited me to attend her Church. I had been looking for the right Church to worship in for some time, knowing that faith was an important part of me, not only through my upbringing as a child but also through school, where good teachers such as Pat answered my many questions about the meaning of life. When I went for the first time, I was struck by how diverse the congregation was, with people from the Caribbean worshipping alongside their white British counterparts. I sensed that it was a very peaceful place. I felt at home immediately. People were very accepting of myself and Philip. It was truly a place where I felt welcome and able to be myself and experience the peace that I needed.

I attended regularly and, as time went by, began to realise that the people I prayed with had become like family to me: mothers, fathers, brothers and sisters. They embraced me and I embraced them; we helped each other when there was need. These friendships meant a great deal to me. The loneliness that I had experienced for a long time finally left me and I learnt that I was not solely in control of my life, but that a greater being, who I believe is God, is very much in charge and that I have to listen for that voice on my journey. I understood that men and women do not ever have to be alone and that no matter what family or community they feel that they may have lost, it is more than possible to regain this closeness with other people. The community that I grew up in may have rejected me but I had found one that was willing to accept me. In 2007 I was baptised; this also gave me strength which I was able to pass on to others.

From 2006 to 2009, I continued to volunteer at KN; during that time Jasvinder would invite me to stand on the platform at her presentations and I would share my story as a survivor. I was also involved in many other areas of KN's work; in 2007, Jasvinder asked me to organise the launch of her second book, 'Daughters of Shame', up in the north of England. I was fortunate to meet the survivors who spoke of their stories, and went on to meet many other important people who campaigned against forced marriages and honour-based violence.

I also had MixTogether. I had a great deal of respect for the work that those disowned, those worried about disownment and those in mixed relationships have kept going on this very real online community. We had created a very important resource, meeting the needs of a large number of people who were not only struggling for family acceptance and in despair but sometimes in real danger. This became a lifeline for many like me. In the early days, I represented MT on platforms which I shared with Jasvinder and publicised MT wherever and whenever I could. On one occasion I recall a discussion on the Asian network radio station, Nihal's programme. Nihal was talking to his radio audience about mixed marriages; there were some pretty fierce arguments about 'going against the family and community' and how these relationships were wrong, no great reason given in my view about why. I phoned in and was unfortunately the last caller on the programme, but I spoke about how culture is transitional, that it does not always stay the same over time, and was pleased to hear that Nihal understood this point. I recall that many people on these programmes had been disowned because their parents did not accept their mixed relationship. Others came on who said that their families had accepted them. It occurred to me that the ones where things had worked out successfully needed to talk with those who were just starting out on the road.

By 2008, a lot of people were posting on MT and many of them became 'regulars'. The more people who came looking for help, the more we realised how much we could give by sharing our own experiences, and in some cases, how lucky we were to have come through. I may not have been successful with my birth family, but I had been successful in new family and my marriage. It also felt good to talk about what happened to us and what we felt about it. I did not want anyone to go through what I went through and tried to give them the guidance I never had. If someone was being forced to choose between their family and their partner, I always encouraged them to do everything they could to reconcile or at least maintain contact with their families unless it was dangerous for them to do so. The men and women who sought our support on the forum were not always in a relationship; sometimes they were having difficulties with their families who tried to prevent them from seeking independence and making their own choices, the issues of shame and honour still the reason for their unhappiness.

The regular posters got to know each other well through the forum and it wasn't long before someone suggested that we all meet up. Although at first there were only a handful of us, we all enjoyed the experience and as time went by we had what we called our 'MT meet-ups' every few months. Sometimes newcomers on the site wanted to talk face-to-face, knowing that they could meet in a safe environment and get real physical support. I began to look forward to these meetings. We would enjoy a meal together and make time and space for people to discuss whatever they wanted. Many came with their partners who had never met anyone in the same situation as themselves before. They were able to share their experiences and give each other support and soon many of them were posting on the forum too, helping others by telling them what they'd learnt and sharing the joy as well as the pain. I valued other times too – sometimes just two of us would meet, enjoying being close and accepted, providing what our families could not. We had no resources to help us fund the meetings but the determination of individuals to get there even when they had very little money touched me deeply. I realised that we all felt this was something we needed to work on, and so we have.

Although I had lost my family and community, meeting with this group of like-minded individuals has shown me that it is possible to create your own community, and this is one that we have developed to help people make a better future for themselves. I am so proud of the non-judgemental approach our members have to individuals from such a wide variety of backgrounds and beliefs. People are genuinely interested in listening and offering support where this is appropriate and needed. MT is a place where everyone is made to feel welcome. It is a lifeline to many who come through it, a community that some pass through fleetingly while others keep in daily contact for months or years until they feel strong enough to cope on their own and leave. Several stay with MT even when they have no need for help any more, and continue to contribute with compassion and wisdom. The MT community forum has gained strength from the examples of people we were able to help, especially in situations that to begin with seemed impossible to resolve. Sometimes we are amazed at the changes that take place. Initially, families treat their son or daughter with silence, dismissal and rejection for months, often years, but with the right approach and help they have been involved in their children's marriages and go on to be loving grandparents to a new mixed-race generation.

Often the stories I read on the forum affect me deeply and I have remained close friends with many people who came to MT. All our stories are different, yet here, we are on common ground. Some of the members have asked me to share their stories with others, in the hope that someone out there will read them and realise that they are not alone. I am glad to do this.

Chapter 11

We Are People of Honour

"There is something beautiful about all scars of whatever nature. A scar means the hurt is over, the wound is closed and healed, done with."

(Harry Crews)

It is a cold winter morning in 2010. I have woken earlier than usual for the last few days because I know the phone could ring at any minute. I have sometimes give my number to women that I have met at various points in my life or on the MixTogether forum, who have asked for help with their situation, people that I know that I can trust and are genuine in their request for help. The young woman whose call I am waiting for on this particular day is an Asian Sikh; she is in a relationship with a white man and has left her family to be with him. I have been worried about her for a few days now; she has phoned me several times over the last few weeks and cries a great deal when she calls. I can hardly make out her words between the sobs and worry that I am missing something she is trying to share with me. I am concerned about her, but when the phone eventually rings that day I am as ready as I can be, reminded of what it was like when I left home all those years ago. I hope that I can hear her today.

"I don't know what to do," she says. "My mum won't see me, I miss my siblings and I want to go back home, but I know they won't have me back, unless I agree to marry..." Her voice trails off and I can hear shuffling on the phone while she tries to compose herself, as she is overwhelmed by her feelings. We go through her situation: she says that she will have to marry the man her parents have chosen for her if they are to accept her back. I ask her if this is what she wants to do. She tells me it isn't. I ask how she would cope with being married to someone that she is not happy with. She is clear that she would be very unhappy as she wants to be with her present partner.

I understand that she needs to talk for a period before she can arrive at a decision, but I am also worried about her safety if she returns home and about the fact that she is not convinced that she would not be forced to do something she does not want to do. We talk about this at length and what would happen if she went home. She tells me that she would just have to get married to someone the family chose. She has an idea of who this might be. She does not want this and it's clear to me that she is most concerned about this. She talks of the many worries she has about her present situation, the lack of support that she has and the lack of understanding, which is why she asked for my telephone number, to talk to someone who had been through a similar experience.

"How did you cope all these years without seeing your family?" she asks and then, "I don't think I can do it..." This is a question that I am often asked, as people want to somehow predict what would happen to them based on someone else's experience in a similar situation. I explain what happened to me, but also that her experience will be hers and not necessarily the same. These questions are an indication of the isolation of the situation for these women in terms of being to find someone who will not be judgemental. They have experienced something of the dynamic of the misplaced notion of honour, having been told that they are shaming their families by wanting to make choices for themselves.

We talk at length about our experiences and I am led by her questions as I realise that this is the important thing for her at this time. I know that many of the women that I have spoken to would like a quick answer as they are in such turmoil. I try to be as honest as I can, at the same time aware of the vulnerability and heartbreaking situation of this young woman.

She asks me more questions, especially about how I dealt with particular things in life without my family. I reassure her that she's not alone in what she is going through; what is happening to her also happened to many others not unlike her, and the things that have happened to her are not things that she has to justify because of the guilt that has been placed on her and that I understand this completely. She thanks me for sharing an important part of my life with her and I thank her for trusting me when she does the same for me. The experience of this is empowering for both of us.

We stay in touch for several months and we both know we have a shared experience that many out there have yet to find; we are grateful and know that even if we lose touch we will never forget one another. I let her know that I will be there if she ever needs me again; this offer to each other is something that I think means a great deal to the many women I have linked with over the years, disowned or shunned by their families. Also I hope that this young woman will know that she now has someone that she can go to who will be reliable and who she can trust, should she need this in future. I keep the channels of communication open and leave it up to them if they want to contact me. Many young women cannot return to their families, despite trying to engage with them, as families simply don't want to know, as I learnt in my situation. For some there is acceptance some years down the line, sometimes with conditions, other times with partial or full integration with their families. Those who do not see their families again often need a lot of help and support.

I visit my friend B, a woman I met through both Karma Nirvana and MixTogether. She and I have cried together about our families a few times. We are sitting in her garden, grateful for the chance to connect and help each other. B is in a mixed relationship like me. She was forced into marriage at seventeen – no choice was given and threats made if she did not comply. She now has a loving and supportive white partner who makes the best nimbu chutney I know. He has reached out to her culture and connected to things that are important to her, which are now important to both of them. We are sitting on garden chairs in our dressing gowns, it is early in the morning and the garden is a very peaceful place to be.

"How do I do it, Simran? Will this empty feeling ever go away?" She cries for her mum, her siblings and her extended family, none of whom want to know her; we reflect and share how we have coped, talking about inner strength and faith.

That day, I am given an amazing example of that strength when she tells me that she and her partner offer respite care to a child with disabilities each week; she talks about her routine which has helped her stay focused and get through each day. She has a job which needs knowledge of IT systems and skill in business negotiations. She has a great ability to form relationships and maintain them, both in her circle of friends and with her partner's family; all this speaks to me of someone who is doing their best despite the rejection that she has faced by leaving her arranged marriage. I realise that B is going to be OK. She is a bright intelligent woman who has found the courage to move her life forward despite the many traumas of her past; I want her to be happy. I am sometimes so sad about the men and women who believe that they have no choice.

I tell B that she reminds me of my sister Ambi, for the good qualities that I saw in Ambi, of a sister's friendship as a child. We hug; B has been more of a sister to me than I could have expected over the many years that mine have not been there. This is when we realise that friends can become the family that we have lost.

She slips in a few jokes which she often does to make me laugh when I get too serious and then she says, "The past is a foreign country – they do things differently there." Her big smile and glistening eyes tell me that this is not just a joke... she is moving on. I laugh with her, knowing all too well what she is saying: that our unhappy past does not have room in our futures.

I call my friend Solome, a Muslim woman I met on MT in the early days of its existence. I enjoy our conversations and am keen to catch up on her news. Solome and I connected from day one for a number of reasons, not least because we had children and husbands and jobs, and felt the isolation of raising children without the full support of our extended families. Solome is married to a Sikh man who she met whilst at university, like so many of the couples who join MT. She used to tell me how much she wanted her family to accept her husband and children and the struggle she had with this, as her family treated her as less than worthy of any connection with them. She also talked about the difficulties of her husband's parents' negative attitude towards their relationship, despite them having had a Sikh wedding. She felt guilty that she had brought this unwanted relationship on her new family and yet her bravery in the struggle for her children's acceptance so that they would know their heritage constantly amazed me. But one thing she could never manage to do was persuade her parents to meet her husband. They were clear that they did not want to see him. This hurt her very deeply and she was concerned that the children would be affected by the division between the families. Her husband was always kind and supportive to her and never said anything to her family about the situation because of his love and respect for his wife; they have remained strong despite these issues. She reminded me of my friend Bimla, the Sikh girl I met in primary school who lived across the road from us, and our innocent friendship which was cut short when her sister ran away to be with her Muslim boyfriend. I knew that having these 'unacceptable' relationships meant that you were no longer part of the family and community and I understood that, for Solome, her struggle to maintain a relationship with her own family was no easy feat. I had the utmost respect for her courage and determination.

Solome and I met regularly over the years, supporting each other and talking about our children and the joy they gave us. We shared laughter and discussions with our children too, protecting them, equipping them with information and also being open with them about their heritage. We answered their questions as best we could and learnt what mattered to them. As a result, our children have become strong in their knowledge and more self assured by knowing who they are and that as parents, we will never force them to do something that is not right for them.

Still, over time, Solome's situation has mellowed; her family now accepts that they cannot walk all over her. She says what she is prepared to tolerate and what she is not; this has taken time and courage to work through. We often talk about taking control of our situations. She went through long periods of not seeing her family and suffered very badly as a result of their rejection, yet she never gave up. She stood her ground and at last the family has accepted her and the children. She meets with them, taking the children to visit. Sadly, her father still won't see her husband; he will not come to her house and her husband is not welcome at the family home, purely because he is a Sikh. Solome and I talk about this and agree that race and religion are the main things that can cut ties between people.

At first, I couldn't help comparing Solome's situation to my own and feeling a little envious – her siblings and mother come to her house and she goes to theirs. *I can only dream of that.* My family cut me out completely and all the doors I tried to open were slammed shut. I miss them all but especially Ambi. I often wondered what she looked like now and what would happen if we met once again. I know how hard Solome has worked at this but don't know what else I could have done to achieve what she has. At first these thoughts distressed me and made me feel different again: *why me?* But now it occurs to me that there are many different types of strengths and weaknesses in families and how they handle relationships varies too. I believe I tried as hard as I could. Through this, I console myself. I do not want to feel the odd one out and to resent people talking about the successes they have had with their own families, and with the help of MT, I can now honestly say that I do not hate my family and I don't dislike myself any more. I am relieved that my sadness has not made me bitter and I genuinely want others to have the best of their families, to try everything they can to maintain their relationships as Solome has.

Some of my friends on MT wanted to tell their stories in their own words. Here is Leena's:

"I was born to Hindu parents in India and raised in the UK. Growing up, things were pretty good. My parents occasionally did have some vicious arguments but for me, as a child, it was an idyllic time. I knew I was loved and I never wanted for anything, and honestly speaking, I was spoiled. However, saying that, the one thing that my parents did not give me freely was independence. When my brother went down to the shops on his own at nine years old, it was acceptable. If I went at nine years old, my brother would have to escort me. I wasn't allowed to go to town on my own, or stay over at friends. It got worse the older I got. My friends would want to meet in town to go shopping – I wasn't allowed to join them. I stopped asking after a while because I knew what my parents' response was going to be. It was only when I started driving that I started to do a lot of these things – however, I always had to answer my phone when my parents rang.

"Boys – ha!" My parents disapproved of me having anyone male in my life barring family. I never told them about my male best friends, or that my female friends had started having boyfriends. I kept my two lives separate which made things difficult at times. I was so lonely watching my friends couple off knowing that although I'd love to have a boyfriend, it would be hard to manage because of my parents.

I grew up – went to university, had crushes, had guys asking me out and I rejected them because I didn't like them enough to go behind my parents' back. Then one day I met this white guy who was cute and smart and I felt comfortable around him. At first, we were just friends, but then we started dating. It was the most wonderful feeling knowing that this amazing guy wanted ME. I fell so deeply in love that I knew that I wanted him for the rest of my life. I kept my relationship quiet from my parents as I knew they would not approve – they'd started talking about finding a husband for me despite my telling them that I was not interested.

Several years later, I got engaged to the guy that I fell in love with. Telling my parents was the hardest thing I ever did. It was horrible. I felt so lonely and so scared and so ashamed because I hadn't even mentioned his name to them in the five years we'd been dating. My parents reacted badly to the news and I won't dwell on what happened. It was the worst year of my life. I was a mess. I spent all my time arguing with my parents to make them see why I loved him and my parents tried anything and everything to drive us apart. I couldn't function and everything slipped away. I started self-harming – my blood pressure rose and I stopped sleeping. I even started thinking about suicide or running away from everyone because I didn't know how to cope. I felt so useless and worse, I was hurting everyone I loved by my selfishness. I was so low that I didn't know what to do until one day I found MixTogether. It was incredible to find a community where everyone understood my pain and where I was coming from – they were people like me. Knowing that I had their support helped me realise that there was so much more to life and that I had a way out. I just had to take it – that I wasn't being selfish for wanting to live life my own way. Slowly, over time, the MT community helped me and my partner to get over that hurdle and grow. I just wish that I'd found MT a lot earlier as it would've helped me from the beginning. I got married to the man I love. I still have a relationship with my parents, albeit very different to how it was previously, and I can put that down to MT's help. I'm happy now. Thank you MT."

Finally, here is P's story, also in her own words;

"I came from a large Punjabi family; we were six sisters and one brother. I was the second eldest and my brother was the youngest. We came to the UK when I was three and my sister was eight. From an early age I was taught the value and importance of boys and would often pray for a brother in front of pictures of Hindu gods on my mother's instructions. I remember how one morning on my way out to school my elder sister was in tears. She had just heard the news that we had another sister, the sixth girl. In school that day I felt very strange as if my sister had told me someone had died.

My father was a factory worker and he strongly believed that all of us should get a good education and get good jobs, not work in a factory like he had to. People in our community were not so ambitious for their daughters and they often mocked my father for his views. These people also pitied us as we had so many girls. My father's status, if you like, was quite low.

Our parents were quite strict and we were not encouraged to have many friends, as friends were seen as a dangerous influence. We had to wear trousers all the time and make-up was forbidden; we couldn't watch some TV programmes in case we saw couples kissing. Also, as we got older, our Indian cinema trips came to an end, I think because they were about romantic love, but we continued to listen to Hindi film music on the radio as a family. Sometimes it felt like we were leading double lives. My parents lived in fear of their children letting them down and we learnt about this early on. We felt that we were a burden to our parents simply because we were girls. We had known about wayward girls who had run away with boyfriends and this was akin to killing your parents.

My older sister was not the academic type but was encouraged to stay on in Sixth Form and get some O-Levels at least, and she managed to get a good job in an office. She had an arranged marriage at the age of twenty one, quite late some people thought. She was happy to go along with the arranged marriage as she felt it was her only way out of a life of restrictions.

I went on to higher education, got my degree and after two years of working, my parents thought it was the right time to be looking for a match for me. I didn't like the idea much but felt the same as my sister, that it was a way out. Then I met S and my life took a different path to what my parents had hoped for. At this time my younger sisters were nineteen, seventeen, sixteen, thirteen and my brother was twelve. I was twenty three and S was thirty six, married with two young children and white. Yes, this was my parents' worst nightmare coming true.

We met in secret and during work hours only, so it was not easy. I didn't tell any of my siblings for fear of them letting it out if I fell out with any of them. After only six months of courting, we were in a serious relationship and knew it was time for me to leave home. My parents became suspicious and things became desperate, and I didn't return home one night. We found a bedsit, and after five days I returned to work. At lunchtime my father came to my workplace and begged me to come home saying, "Everything will be fine, we know you are seeing this man. Just wait for his divorce and you can get married to him. Let's do this properly." I was quite naïve and believed what he said. I didn't feel too good about living with S unmarried and wanted my parents' blessing more than anything. So I went back home but it was a different story when I got through the door. They said it was best that I "forget him as no damage has been done," i.e. no one knows yet. That was their biggest fear, that it would get out in to the community who would say, "We told you so. We told you it was a mistake to educate girls." My parents' world fell apart. They said, "How dare you throw this in our faces after all we have done for you. You were our piece of gold and now look what you have done." They were concerned for my sisters not getting any marriage offers because of my actions. My father said, "If you leave this house you cannot come back." My mother said she would have a heart attack and die if I left. They made me swear that I would not leave home again. I did it knowing full well that I would leave again. I had to lie as there was no reasoning with them.

In the next few days, there was talk that I would be going to India with my mum but this didn't ring alarm bells for me as I was still very trusting. Then one Sunday afternoon I could hear my mother in the other room crying out loudly that she knew I was planning to leave again. Not able to face any more rantings, I took the plunge and quickly stepped out of the house with a ten pence coin in my hand, just wearing my Punjabi suit and 'chappals' (Indian style sandals). I am a little ashamed and also saddened and angry that I was forced to literally run away. With my heart pounding and body full of fear, I ran as fast as I could to a nearby cul-de-sac and knocked on a house where a retired couple believed my story of being lost and let me use their phone. Within ten minutes or so, a good friend came to pick me up. I lay in the back of the car with a blanket over me as she said she had seen my brother-in-law at the top of the road. She took me to her mother's house, ten minutes away. Then S came to get me and we started our life together. When we got in our house that evening, I called home and spoke to my dad. He said, "Come home, Daughter, just come home," but I said, "No, I'm not coming home," and I put the phone down. He sounded desperate and upset and I feel bad about that now, but at the time I was angry with what they had put me through. A part of me believed my mother *would* die as a result of me leaving but I was prepared for that. I just had a strong belief that they couldn't do this to me and it was my time to lead my own life.

A few weeks into our life together, I wrote a letter home which came back to me with words such as "You are not our sister, do not contact us." A cousin got in touch and asked me what was I doing acting like a white woman and I should go back to my family. A few months later, I plucked up the courage to phone home and speak to my mother. It was a brief call where she was abusive about S and said I should just stay with the white community. It was these rejections that I found hardest to deal with. I was in a state of sadness for much of my first year with S. I believed that over time I would be accepted by my family but that time never came. I went to the house once and my mother very forcefully told me she would gladly kill me. I was filled with guilt and sadness that I had lost my family.

It was very strange to go from a big family to being on your own. I always made a mental note of any family birthdays but didn't send any cards in case I would anger or hurt them. Now I think I should have sent the cards; so what if they threw them away, at least they would have seen I was showing I still cared. I missed my family terribly in the early years. I would drive over late at night, park nearby so I could just see comings and goings and once I saw my brother come home from school carrying a large musical instrument and I felt really sad that I couldn't be a part of his growing up. I carried on writing the odd letter but never had any replies. Each time I would get my hopes up only to find rejection. I found this painful and hard to take.

I went again to my parents' house just after my fortieth birthday. I was feeling now was a good time to try again. My father said, "You are not welcome here," and went off to sit in his car. My mother came out and said tearfully that I had caused my sisters a lot of difficulty and she joined her hands and said she prayed that I was happy in my life and then closed the door on me. That was quite hard to take. Here was a woman who had been ruled by her husband all her life, I could see she really did love me but was powerless to do anything about it.

As the years went on, I began to get angry at my family. How could they do this to their own flesh and blood? They just don't have a concept of unconditional love. My siblings are still influenced by what my father says. They are all carrying this little secret around with them, that they have disowned their daughter and sister. We have all lost out on many years. I've missed out on watching my parents grow into old people and my siblings from teenagers into middle age. What a waste.

And now it is twenty five years that I haven't been in touch with any of my family. S has been very understanding and supportive throughout. At the time of our meeting, his marriage was not in good shape so this made things a little easier. Being a stepmum to two young boys when you have just lost your own family was a tough call. I must admit I did not handle it well at all. The boys were lovely towards me though and now they are adults they babysit our four children. They all get on really well, so something good has come out of our struggles. S's parents and sisters were supportive right from the beginning which gave us a feeling of being normal. Once S's parents wrote a letter to my father asking him to reconsider his actions but my father returned the letter to them with the message to "Leave us alone."

At times I feel angry that my parents' decision to disown me has denied my children a rich cultural heritage, not to mention missing out on a large extended family. But these are my worries and although my children are curious about my family, they don't feel they are missing out in any way. It is hard to keep it alive by yourself. We do what we can. We cook Indian food, listen to the music and watch the films. We have sometimes gone to the Gurdwara. I don't want my children growing up thinking that Asian people are weird or alien to them. We even went on a trip to India. I had in my mind that they would experience an idyllic village life and live with a family that would treat them as their own; they would be free to play with other children and maybe learn some Punjabi.

I tried a few contacts but nobody was willing to see me, so we had a nice time doing the tourist trail! It was very strange going back to the country of your birth and not experiencing the real India. I hope one day it will be possible.

I try not to dwell on the hurt and anger. My husband and our four children are my family now and that is my future and the past is just memories. If by some miracle my parents and siblings want me in their lives then that would be great, but I am done with looking for a family as I have my own family now."

These are just a few of the many stories that people have shared with me over the years, mainly from friends I made on through MixTogether website. I often think how incredibly honoured and privileged I am to have known so many 'survivors' and sadly, some who feel like 'victims'. I acknowledge that this is the experience that they have had but am careful not to call them either of these names if they do not want to be associated with them. Sometimes men and women want the chance to continue with their lives without these labels to remind them of what happened to them. These are honourable people in my mind, who have had the enormous courage to take action and do things for themselves despite their painful memories. I know that people do not always feel they have been courageous: many of them miss their families and at times experience the guilt of having to go against the authority of parents, despite them being adults in their own right. They often long for a family reunion and all that goes with it. However, even if they don't realise it, they have needed courage in order to continue, to get out of the 'forced' life situations or live without the misguided sacrifices that their families required them to make. I am aware from my own experiences that many more are still trying to make it and take control of their lives, still living with some of the oppressive practices that take away their right to choose, and sometimes the right to life itself.

I hope these stories will help many others to see that they are not alone and that by sharing them, a small voice may be heard and acknowledged by us all. I know that this would have been so important to me in the early part of my journey and hopefully it might be for others who read these accounts.

Chapter 12

In Search of Healing: Rwanda

"Coming generations will learn equality from poverty, and love from woes."

(Khalil Gibran)

I n 2009, I was given the opportunity to travel to Rwanda in central Africa. It had been fifteen years since the genocide which left thousands of children orphaned and homeless, and a good friend of mine through Church, Jemrose, was working out there, setting up a home for orphans. I was keen to go over and lend a hand. I asked her if she would mind a visit from me and she agreed to this, saying she would enjoy my company. The aim was for me to support her in any way I could which including doing some fundraising before I went: this would go towards setting up the home and buying some of the equipment they needed. Jemrose's project was something I really wanted to support; I often wondered about the suffering of the Rwandan people and what it must be like to have everything you love taken away – your family, your home, every person that you have known in your life. I wanted to know how people survived in those situations and what it was they needed most, so that we could provide the best help.

I started to prepare for my journey: I did the fundraising by cooking for colleagues at work, I had help from friends with some of the equipment we needed to purchase and I saved up enough of my own money for the cost of travel and staying with Jemrose. I decided to go for a month to make it worthwhile and took time off from work. My journey to Africa was also very important in another way: this would be the first time that I had returned to the land of my birth and the place where my parents spent eighteen years of their lives, albeit in Kenya. I spent a lot of time thinking about them, trying to recall what it was like growing up there, although I wasn't even three when we left. I remembered hearing them talk in Swahili with their Kenyan friends and this conjured up poignant, long-forgotten memories of the culture and food. This was all very much in my mind as I made my plans to go to Rwanda via Kenya.

I also felt that this was a time when I was the strongest I had been in many years. I had been through counselling and a long time had passed since I'd had any contact with my family. Perhaps such a visit would help me understand how fortunate I was and be able to do something for someone else at the same time. I hoped that I might learn from this and that it would help me make sense of the gift of life. I researched Rwanda thoroughly before I went: the genocide, the history, everything I could lay my hands on. It wasn't a place that you went without some worry, as there were still troubles. I would also be travelling abroad on my own for the first time and where we were going was not easy to get to. When the time came for me to leave Britain, I was filled with a mixture of excitement and trepidation.

There is a girl – a teenager – who is always hanging around the bus pick-up point, near Kigali airport, begging for small change and a hug if one is going. Jemrose and I are walking back to her house in the heat of the late afternoon when we see her. Jemrose says she doesn't know if this girl has anywhere to live and I ask if it's OK to give her some change – I'm not sure what the organisation's policy is on these things. She says it is up to me, fine if I feel I want to do it. The girl smiles at us – I think she recognises me as we have passed by several times before. She comes over and asks for some change which I give her and as I do, I put my arms out to her to show acceptance, that I want to know her. She is warm, wrapped in a shawl, but she is barefoot. Her feet are cracked and hard from walking on the dusty floor. It means a great deal to me to have met her. She could be a princess, a daughter, a sister. I am meeting 'sisters' on a frequent basis these days, in Africa as well as at home! There are many such people that I meet, they often say, "You are welcome to Rwanda!" Despite everything that has happened to them and their country, they are not bitter, still welcoming those who mean well.

Rwanda is a beautiful place. It is known as The Land of a Thousand Hills and Kigali is a city built on some of those hills. The land is very green and the housing and general infrastructure is much improved over the years since the genocide. However, poverty is clear to see too. For most, having just one meal a day is the norm and some don't even get this: I go on to meet many people in the local community who are struggling to survive. The provision of water and electricity are constant struggles for many and I am reminded how even for Jemrose, water can be a costly commodity and not easily available. Living with these conditions is a welcome challenge for me, as – not unlike many back at home in Britain – I have taken such essentials for granted.

The house I am staying in while I am here is Jemrose's home for orphans. It is a French style ex-colonial place that she has repaired and painted. Ever since I arrived we have been busy, buying furniture, organising the kitchen pantry, setting up tables and chairs in the lounge, and in the evening I stitch old sheets by hand for the beds: at least my poor sewing is useful for something.

We realise that the run down garden includes an orchard with mango and banana trees. I cook Indian food and learn that there are now culinary links between Rwandans and Indians, for instance Rwandans also make roti. I am helping Jemrose organise projects for young people which will support them through their education, house them in the school holidays and provide respite care for those who need it. Some are referred to Jemrose through her links with the community, especially those who are living in difficult situations and who need love and care in a safe environment. I find myself enjoying the time we spend with these young people and how little is needed to improve their situation a great deal. The kindness and understanding that people need is found in Jemrose.

Over the last few days, my visits to the JAM orphanage and the Kigali Genocide Memorial Centre have opened my eyes to the atrocities that were committed in 1994. Nearly a million people were killed in a war that was about ethnic and tribal differences, fuelled by ignorance, hatred and greed. The Memorial Centre also commemorated other Holocausts in history, having a huge effect on me; it is almost impossible to imagine that the bodies of over 250,000 victims are buried here. There is a special Children's Memorial which is dedicated to "*the memory of the many thousands of children whose lives were so cruelly and intentionally cut short*". It is heartbreaking but also uplifting: the Memorial Centre has an education department which acts as a resource for the new national curriculum, supporting 'civic education'; its aim is also to examine the lessons that can be learnt from this and other genocides so they will not be repeated and to teach about human rights and responsibilities. As we stand on the hill where the memorial is built, I see a coffin crowned with flowers being taken down to the mass grave area and Jemrose tells me that sometimes the bones of relatives are found all these years later and the burial allows people to come and grieve and pay their respects. I know I will never forget this place where so many Rwandans – both Hutus and Tutsis – lost their lives in a mindless massacre: it will remain engraved on my mind. I am also finding it difficult to understand how God could let this happen – it is a challenge to my faith. We often pass a large Church on our travels. Jemrose tells me that it served as a refuge for many during the genocide crisis but one day everyone inside it was shot; I am filled with sadness, as a Church is a place I always associate with peace. I am angry and confused, again asking, "*Why would God allow this?*" I find it hard to deal with this side of humanity and can't understand how people can be so intentionally cruel to each other. I come to the conclusion that such evil acts cannot be explained and it is not within my capacity to understand.

I am at the local market with Jemrose when we meet a woman who has helped with some negotiations within the community. She comes to visit us and tells us her story. She says that one day during the genocide she walked amongst the bodies looking for survivors and found a young child on the road who was crying for its mother. She picked up the child and said, "I am your mother now". This is one of many stories I hear which help me to appreciate how fortunate I am. I do not have to live with the fear and devastation that these people still experience on a daily basis. Their traumas have continued long after the genocide: they have little sense of security, have to endure great hardships and have few prospects in life unless they get an education which most cannot afford. I realise how lucky I am to live in Britain where children can go to school without having to pay: the children I meet here are thirsty for knowledge and very enthusiastic, wanting to do well; they value education and consider it very important and an honour, even from a young age.

I stay in an orphanage called the Fred Nkunda Centre in Gitarama for a few days. I learn much from this time about the life of orphans and those supporting them. On entering the centre, I am touched to see slabs engraved with names of people from all over the world, who have contributed in many ways to the upkeep of this orphanage. Jemrose and I go to the classes that the children attend in the daytime and see first-hand the difficulties of young people who are disabled or have learning needs. Many of them are put in classes with the smaller children even though their needs are different because they are older. I see that the buildings are very sparse and equipment is always needed for the young people staying here. There is a sewing class and pottery class which inspire me. I spend the last of my money on half a cow which is turned into a meal for the whole orphanage – meat is expensive to buy and at best, a once-a-month treat; I still have enough left to buy some drinks and sweets – a bottle of Fanta for each child is provided and is a rare treat. The time I spend here has quite an impact on me. The centre is very well run and the staff are amazing, often not financially well off themselves, yet giving up their lives to help these children, becoming mothers and fathers to them even though many of the helpers have lost their own parents and close family. In this place there is spirit and laughter and once again I realise how much I appreciate my present family's love and support, how fortunate I am not to have to think about where my next meal is coming from, and to feel safe, amongst many other things. I recall the spiritual connection with our Christian faith in the morning assembly, and how this unites us, whoever and wherever we are.

I get on well with Jemrose's adopted son Dieudonné, who is now in his twenties. I learn his story gradually: his first language is Kinyarwanda, but he has some English and it doesn't need many words for me to understand the horror of what he has been through. Jemrose explained that he was orphaned at a very young age when he witnessed the massacre of his whole family. He managed to escape by running into the forest where he hid, lying motionless for many hours at a time in exactly the same spot, for three months. When he finally got up, his body was bent; he could no longer stand straight after hiding in fear for so long. He was one of the many children who finally ended up at the orphanage at the Fred Nkunda Centre in Kigali, all of whom had suffered in similar ways. Jemrose worked at the centre from time to time and she ended up adopting him. I am humbled by Dieudonné: despite his loss, he appreciates life. He works hard at his job, yet gets up early each day with a self-discipline that I envy because he likes to get the house clean before he goes to work. Sometimes I find him brushing the dust off our shoes, selflessly doing these things with pride: his love of Jemrose is clear for all to see. He calls me "Auntie". I have never been called that, despite being one; he makes me feel like a member of his family. Yet again I am reminded how lucky I am. I have a husband and children who love me, a good job, I have never struggled financially in a way that many have to. All thoughts of the loneliness that I felt at having no birth family connection are put into perspective when I hear Dieudonné's story; his attitude to life particularly affects and inspires me – despite losing everything in such a brutal way, he has grown up to be kind, generous, unselfish and cheerful. I also notice that he sometimes has difficult days and Jemrose shares how hard it is for both of them at times, but as my time in Rwanda comes to a close, I believe that of all the people I have known in my life, it is Dieudonné who has taught me the most. His survival gives me reason to survive. I understand how much greater his loss is than mine and, unlike me, he had no choice: others determined his fate for no logical or purposeful reason. Although I can see parallels with missing my own family it can never compare with the loss that he and other people like him have experienced. As we drive around, I notice plaques and banners with slogans saying, "We must forgive but not forget." I think of my parents and the rest of my family and know that I have forgiven them and will never forget them. I have had my life and faith challenged during this trip but it has also been strengthened in surprising ways.

As my departure date draws nearer, I find that I am reluctant to leave. I say to Jemrose that it's no problem for me to stay a bit longer, even if this isn't strictly true, but if I could have, I would have done. She reminds me that I have a family at home who need me. I know this but right now it seems to make more sense for me to be doing something in Rwanda than returning to Britain. I know that if it wasn't for Philip and the children, at that moment I might have chosen to do something very different with my life.

When I arrive back in England, Philip and the kids are there to meet me at the airport and it is wonderful to see them. I take a while to recover but after a few days Philip remarks that this is the first time he has seen me so calm — spiritually, emotionally, in every way. I realise that the people of Rwanda have helped me to heal. I have them to thank. I am more at peace. I try to explain to Philip the sense of community I found in Rwanda; despite the hardship, people would still do whatever they could to help one another. They survived through working together, otherwise they would not eat or have any support. So many of the people I met were warm and had a richness in their lives that I rarely saw anywhere else, an acceptance yet always striving to find a solution, never giving up on the struggle to survive. Still laughter, despite their circumstances. Yet they had lost more than most of us can imagine.

Whenever I have difficult times, I think of the people I met in Rwanda, knowing that they would do everything they could in order to survive, because they have to, and not just helping themselves but others as well. I remember everyone singing together early in the morning in the many churches around the city on the hills and how their sense of spirit was not broken by the most appalling circumstances.

After many years of grieving for my family, I know there is nothing more I can do to bring them back to me now, but I can do something about the rest of my life and how I spend it. I am thankful for my life and the relationships I have. My journey to Rwanda was a breakthrough in me that said I could survive with God at my side. I have found a new meaning to the term 'family': it is more than flesh and blood. I now have a wider family in my life which is very important to me. I am indebted to Jemrose for allowing me this experience with the open heart that she has.

Chapter 13

A Ghost From The Past

*"There is nothing like returning to a place that remains unchanged
to find the ways in which you yourself have altered."*

(Nelson Mandela)

I t is February 2010. I am pushing a shopping trolley around Medina Stores, an Asian supermarket on the other side of the city. The trolley is full to overflowing: I don't make this trip in my car very often so when I do, I stock up on all the foods and spices we love that I can't get in my local store.

It is a task I am ambivalent about. As I take what I need off the shelves, my movements are measured and my actions are considered carefully, especially if there are local Asian men and women around who might stop me to ask who I am or what my background is, and who indeed is my family? This has happened to me before, it is not unusual in a neighbourhood such as this. Women who shop alone, not wearing their traditional dress and unknown in the community, are watched closely in some of these shops. People like to know who women belong to and what community they are from. Like many survivors of situations like mine, even after all these years I am still watchful, although I avoid eye contact. I had to get used to this in the years after my family disowned me when I became independent. Thirty two years on and subconsciously I protect myself, knowing that I could be hurt by an inappropriate look or an awkward question. At times the desire to make a connection with people who speak my mother tongue is very strong. I long to talk about the foods that I enjoyed as a child, the ingredients for a certain Asian dish, but I have become accustomed to the tell-tale signs. Sometimes, though, there is a good atmosphere; on such days I can help people find what they are looking for and we exchange recipes and talk about the various ingredients in more than one language: these things mean something to me still and it is a way of keeping a link to my cultural roots. It is, after all, something that my father did when I accompanied him to these shops.

I check my shopping list – I don't need much more today; I balance the trolley with its rickety wheels under a large canopy outside the store where an array of fresh fruit and vegetables is on display. I am struck by an Indian-looking woman whose dyed golden-brown hair is tied up in a bun as I do mine some days. I know the figure immediately, even though her back is turned towards me while the assistant helps her with a box of green bhindi, or 'ladies' fingers'. She looks round. I am frozen to the spot, in a state of high alert, waiting for my instincts to kick in, whatever they may be at this time – a time you rehearse for years when you think of meeting someone from your past and what you might say to them and more than this, what they will say to you.

The woman's eyes open wide in recognition and shock. "Oh my God," she whispers. It is Ambi.

She has aged; in those few seconds, I take everything in – her hair thinning along the top of her forehead, clothes immaculately fitted, make-up applied with precision, lipstick still fresh despite the time of the day, four in the afternoon.

I am unable to think straight. I look at her and can't believe this is happening. Am I to have this long-awaited audience with my sister? My sister, Ambi? My image is mirrored in her deep dark eyes, long face, a wave in the hair, small hands. She motions the assistant to leave the bhindi on the shelf for now, then walks around the boxes of vegetables, coming towards me.

"Let me give you a hug!" she exclaims.

I step back, not knowing if I can cope with this. "I...don't know....I don't know who you are..." I say in confusion, my feet stuck to the cold concrete floor of the supermarket, tears stinging my eyes.

Ambi stops. "We are sisters," she says. "Well, I've always thought we are."

I don't know what to say. It is too sudden. Emotions I have buried for so long rush to the surface – anger, love, sadness, longing. I dare not speak in case these emotions spill out and cause her to run away.

I am anxious, and terrified that she will suddenly disappear again. That I won't cope. She is talking, too fast it seems, telling me about her life, her family, her achievements. I search for some reciprocal emotion in her face but there is none. I stand open-mouthed while she flits from one subject to another – it's like we're discussing the vegetables in the supermarket. Ambi has no thought for what it may be like for me and my children without the support that she has clearly had. I try to say something but my words have no effect; the more I try, the more she flits. I don't want to make her angry – in the past she would use anger to communicate and then she would walk away. Most of my memories of Ambi are of her walking away from me, even as a child in the playground, or down the street, or away from family friction,

266

saving herself without a backward glance at her siblings. I don't want her to walk away again – I am wondering if it is too much to expect that this time, things will be different. I feel like a small animal, nervously waiting for this larger animal to decide whether it will eat me up or pass me by. I want to believe that it will not harm me and might even stay for a while, in harmony with me.

She is talking about our past and I listen closely to what she says. Her position is clear: she is sorry, yet is not clear what she is sorry about, she cannot be specific. What I hear is laced with excuses; she mentions the secret affair with her boyfriend and I know then that the reason for her rejection of me is that she could not bear the thought that I knew so much; what I knew was too dangerous, even though I promised I would never tell anyone and never did. (Even now, I have changed her real name so as not to give her secret away.) To protect herself, she had to make me out to be the 'bad one'; she expresses this without any reservation, reeling off statements and generalisations about the differences between 'East' and 'West', what's good and what's bad, saying that I made choices which I was not supposed to make – that I should not have chosen independence and an education away from home, to have married the partner of my choice. While I am taking all this in, she tells me that her daughter has been to university and is herself independent and not living at home. *What did I do that was so different?* I wonder. She tells how she regrets the marriage that was arranged for her at such an early age by our parents and is upset that she was not given the chance to go to university. She confides that hers was not a good childhood.

While she speaks, I try to work out how I feel and how to express this but it is hard, as Ambi is stopping the flow of any communication between us. I realise that what she believes in could well have kept my family away from me – acting as a gatekeeper – and her excuses for disowning me suggest that she does not love me as a sister. I know what sisters do for each other. She does not speak as though we are sisters, does not acknowledge this relationship. She is talking at me, not to me, defending herself – yet I am sure she knows the truth, deep down inside. I look at this woman and all I can see is my beloved older sister who I was once in awe of. How these relationship terms confuse and upset me; they are terms that I cannot use lightly any longer. For me, the word 'sister' implies a sacred connection between one sibling and another. I believe I did my best to fulfil my side of that sacred bargain.

For forty minutes, I stand and listen to her, willing her not to go despite the pain she is inflicting on me with her words. I wait for her to say that she wants to meet my children – her nephew and niece – who are now on the cusp of adulthood; that she wants to know about me and my family, where I live, what I do, what happened to us, how we as a family coped in the aftermath of my disownment. She seems to have no awareness of how I might be feeling, or she doesn't care. It's ironic that throughout my career, I have been trained to understand and deal with the dynamics involved in situations like this but I'm rooted to the spot, unable to communicate. I am terrified that if Ambi and I cannot connect in some way now, I will never have the chance again; yet she won't let me in.

"Well, I'd better be off to finish my shopping," she says suddenly, glancing at her watch. "You never know, we might bump into each other again." With that, she is gone.

I realise I am in shock. I stand for a while, watching her disappear. It feels as though I am losing her all over again so I start to follow her as she wanders from aisle to aisle, picking up the foods of our childhood. She sees me following her, but the cold presence of her back meets me each time, as she chooses to ignore me.

I am remembering Mamaji and Papaji, Noor, Jay, Dev and all the family from when I was young. I know that the thing I miss is belonging to a family: whatever kind of family it is does not matter. I watch her as the previous rejections by her of me come flooding back again. It occurs to me that I cannot run after her like this, acting as if I am begging for her to know me. Eventually I leave the trolley and walk back to my car. I am trying to concentrate very hard on getting back home – to think straight is very difficult. I did not realise that I would react in this way.

I am unwell for many weeks after seeing Ambi. It is hard to describe how your emotional health is connected to your physical well-being at a time like this, but it is. I am anxious and the meeting has left me unsettled, unable to think or do anything with focus. This is a long way from how I like to be. I am protecting my feelings and trying to hard to get over things, only to find that I needed the time to feel normal again. I think of the survivors that I have met and how their lives are impacted, and how they have to pick themselves up without the support of a partner or anyone else for that matter. Dr Lott is understanding, and the only person I can turn to. I know that some things in my life will take longer to heal and that I have done well to have healed as far as I have, and should not beat myself about this.

One thing that helps is writing: when I came back from Rwanda I started to write down my experiences and found that the anger and bitterness I felt was removed from inside me as I wrote, as had happened after counselling years before. I decide that I need to write to Ambi and will risk going to see her with my letter. I need to confront her once and for all, to get the answers to what happened between us, why she had reacted as she had done, rejecting me. I had never wanted to cause 'shame' to the family by knocking on doors, at the same time embarrassing myself again when doors were closed. I do not want to upset and involve her family but she told me that her children were in higher education or work and her husband working abroad so I am hoping she will be home on her own when I go. I wonder how she has explained my situation to them, whether her children know about their cousins. I think carefully about what I will write: this is probably the only chance I will have to ask my questions and explain the events of my life from my point of view.

I make a start, telling her how I felt throughout my childhood and what it was like not being part of the family's rites of passage: the deaths of my parents, the births of my nephews and nieces, their marriages and the arrival of their own children. I leave out the things that I would not want others in her family to pick up on, as the letter might be seen by them; I do not want to say anything about the impact of her relationship with her boyfriend as we had kept that a secret, although it had clearly impacted on me as well as her. I had never knocked angrily on her door demanding to be heard, I never wanted to create a scene in front of her extended family and anyway, they all made it clear that I would never be welcome, that I would never be listened to.

Now is the time for me to have my say. This is a chance for me to break that silence and talk about the things that no one from my birth family has wanted to hear before. If this is all that I can achieve, it will be enough: I will have set the record straight. I know that I am stronger now and can do this. I'm not afraid of their reprisals any more.

It takes me several days to write and when it is finished I ask my friend Jemrose, who is here in Britain on a visit from Rwanda, to read it. I trust her: she knows my deepest thoughts and fears through the counselling that she has provided. She also agrees to come with me when I take it to the house where Ambi used to live and where I hope she still is, some two miles from where I now live (even though Ambi is not aware of this). As I walk down the street, every detail is familiar to me even though it's twenty one years since I've been here. No one is home when I knock. I am nervous but know I have to do this, for my children if not for me. I stare at the door and it feels like a wall between me and my past and at the same time, a physical connection between me and Ambi. In the end, I drop the letter through the letter box and we leave.

In the weeks that follow, I keep wondering if Ambi has received my letter and if so, what her reaction is and whether she will reply. At times I feel it is a hopeless situation, that I should not expect anything from her, but I still keep my sense of dignity: I have broken the silence, whether she reads it or not. It is a freeing act.

I did not put my home address on the letter just in case – I am still conscious of our safety – but have given my email address. One day, there is a message from someone whose email I don't recognise. I open it and begin to read; it is from Ambi's daughter, my niece, written on behalf of her mother. My first reaction is that it is a cowardly thing for Ambi to do, asking her daughter to reply on her behalf; but then again, it was a cowardly act to disown me and my family, so what else would I expect? The email is a painful and very muddled read for me. It is full of excuses for why I was disowned, safeguarding my sister's position and I think what she said would have shocked even my parents. Ambi has mentioned certain things said in our childhood and things that were said to her by her in-laws; she says that she had confronted her mother-in-law about her, Ambi, 'being made' to give up her sister. Had she accepted that so easily? Could she not have tried to put things right between us after all this time that has gone by? I feel that she is still stuck in the past and unwilling or unable to move on, despite the fact we are now women in our fifties. Does she still believe that it is so unforgivable to leave home to start a new life, to try to make a success of what you do, to choose your own partner, all the things she defines as 'wrong'? I wonder if the elders in the community still ask her and the rest of my siblings questions about me and my whereabouts. I am sure that the stigma of the 'runaway daughter' still affects them. A sudden memory comes to me as I read: it is over twenty five years ago but still so clear and painful. On a rare visit to my family home, Dev showed me a photo album of family photographs, many from our childhood. As he turned the pages, I saw that every picture of me had been cut out.

I read on. My niece stresses that even after all this time she is surprised that I would even want to know them. She says this is all a little too late for them now; I know from this that she is caught between her parents' lack of compassion and anger, and my own family, and I know that she is in a difficult position, as I would imagine that it is a case of believing her mother or me, reading between the lines. *What else can she do?* I think to myself. She wrote on behalf of her mother and herself, not aware of what her mother had really done, I had not mentioned her mother's history with me. I have no anger for her, just sadness that my love for my niece is not allowed to flourish, and most of all that she has not been able to know her cousins Adam and Ami, who know of her from me in no negative way, have seen photos of her and heard that she meant a great deal to me. She has blocked me from replying to her email and it is clear that she does not want to know me when I try to connect with her on Facebook. I do not pry any further or try again, and respect that she cannot respond to me now. I think that indeed, shame travels from one generation to the next.

As I close the email, I feel strangely calm. I gave Ambi the chance to reconnect with me, to put the past behind us, but she did not want this. Between the lines, I read that it is too hard for her to engage with what happened in the past and to move on from there, a relationship with me is too difficult; she says that she can't make the 'others' (my siblings) want to know me either.

It is clear that she would not be able to know me and possibly jeopardise her relationships with my other sibling – or is this just an excuse for her bitterness of what life has been for her? Is her life so cosy now that the inclusion of me, my children and Philip would disrupt her life? Whatever it is, it is clear that Ambi is making excuses for not wanting to see me and that this is connected with many things – cowardice, misplaced notions of honour and shame included – but also that human emotions and actions are very complex. I wonder if she can feel this negative emotion or notion of shame, or the pain that this will cause my new family, and whether she has explained this to her children and indeed, how she views her responsibility to also explain this to my children?

The chance for her to free my children from generations of pain caused by my family? I feel for families like mine, including those on MixTogether and those I met in other areas of my work. In the days that follow, I know that these events have finally brought a closure to my relationship with Ambi and through her, the rest of my extended family.

I realise that my disownment has spanned some thirty two years, and that I can no longer keep trying to build bridges with the family through these sporadic events, both inside myself or in any practical way.

I know that I have felt anger about her actions in the past; it would not be normal for me to be otherwise in the face of such rejection – I am only human and not perfect – just like Ambi; the difference is that my anger is gone.

I am still sad, but I am doing my best to forgive, trying to put into practice what I learnt in Rwanda – that forgiveness is only possible when we fully understand the complex behaviour of those that desperately need to survive.

Chapter 14

Belonging

"And now these three remain: faith, hope and love."

(I Corinthians 13:13)

I am sitting on the pier with a notebook in my hand, writing. I am on holiday on the Cornish coast. I look up and see a group of people on the beach below looking relaxed and happy. A dark-haired young woman is standing in the sea, waves splashing against her legs, looking quite the part in her sunglasses and an outfit that is something you might see in a glossy magazine advert for the right gear to wear this summer. She is strikingly beautiful. Circling her is a young man, a little older, who seems intent on getting her to have fun; he kicks up the water and she screams, although there is laughter in her voice, a tone of affection; it is obvious this is someone she knows well. Not far away from them is a handsome older man, silver hair cropped very short and glistening in the bright sunshine, warm sun-baked face glowing, watching protectively, although he joins in the laughter and waves at them.

I close my eyes and let the sun warm my face, listening to the seagulls and the conversations of people who pass. I hear two women talking, saying how similar we become to our mothers as we age. I soak the sun up and feel my thoughts go to my mother; I then take off my shoes and look down at my feet. I think, these remind me of the feet of my mother, rounded and wide with four tiny toes next to one very dominant one. Yes, I am happy that they are like my mother's feet.

It occurs to me that these days I am thinking a lot about my Mamaji and Papaji, two people that I realise I knew for only a very short time in my life – really only my first eighteen years. They did what they could do for me and I am sure they believed they were doing their best. I am thankful to them for giving me the genes of determination and strength of will that enabled me to make something of my life. I realise that this would not have been possible if I had not found my own path, albeit not knowing what would happen to me, albeit without a plan. My father and mother were part of three different worlds during their lives, having taken from and contributed to India, Kenya and then England. They had to adjust to different races, traditions, religions and cultures. I realise that they also gave me the same courage they needed to adapt and change, to find hope where I didn't think there would ever be any, to take the risk with people around me, to believe in the good and just, and give things a try.

I look up at the family group on the sand and think I have over-compensated in many ways with my kids, because at times I felt guilty about their right to an extended family which I could not give them. As parents, Philip and I will have our own challenges with our family, I am in no doubt of that. I worried about my children's future as all parents do, and talked with them about looking after each other. Was this enough? At times in my mind, I hear the cry of the elders in my community that blood is thicker than water and we cannot survive without our family: this had been ingrained in me at one time. I realise now, however, that my children are proving that unconditional love and support can come from close friends as well as family. I tell other mixed couples that this is what happens, that our children experience their world differently to how I experienced my past and my world, and that we can be encouraged by the hope that exists for all families. I think of the struggle it has been to get to where I am now and try not to beat myself up too much about all that. Life has been good to me, God has been good, I have everything I could possibly want and I don't just mean materially. I know that my daughter has had more choices than I could ever have imagined and am proud to be the mother of this girl who can freely voice her opinion without fear, who knows her own mind and most of all, I hope, knows that her mum is 100% there for her, will respect her point of view and will never disown her. My son and I are also very close; he too has been raised as a free spirit and has turned into a young man that I am sure my father would have been proud to know. I joke about how his grandfather would have arm wrestled with him and I tell him about Papaji's spiritual quest for happiness. I see that they are not unlike each other in terms of their faith. I realise that Papaji and Mamaji are still connected to us and the generations to come. We are indeed reclaiming our heritage.

The sea is coming in at high tide and as I close the notebook in which I have been writing down the finishing touches for my story, the little group that I have been watching comes towards me, silhouetted against the setting sun. They are holding hands. As they get closer, I see their smiling faces; they wave to me and I stand to greet them: my daughter Ami, now nineteen, my son Adam, twenty two, and my husband Philip. They kiss me as if we had not seen each other for an eternity. I put my arms around them and we hug, then brush the sand off each others' feet before going back to our rented cottage where we will eat together and talk about the day we have just enjoyed. They ask how my writing is going and I tell them; I am so grateful that they have given me their blessing to share my story, which after all is theirs as well.

This is my family. In this moment of closeness and peace, the turmoil of the past is forgotten but the people who I still think about each day without fail are not and never will be. They are, however, forgiven and wished well, each and every one of them.

I thank God for all that He has done in my life.

I am at peace.

Epilogue

Reflection and Learning

"We shall not cease from exploration and the
end of all our exploring
Will be to arrive where we started and know
the place for the first time."
(Little Gidding: T. S. Eliot)

I have told my story from the beginning, returning in my mind to the places of my childhood, my parents' journeys to Africa, India and then Britain. I took myself back to places where I had been when I heard a particular story about my parents' lives, and also to the perceived wisdom of the elders which we had no reason to believe was not true. The sights, sounds and smells came back as I relived my journey, some parts joyful and others full of sadness and pain. I have felt like a traveller, looking at my family history and upbringing through my fifty two year old eyes with the benefit of hindsight.

It has helped me see more clearly what the family went through and why they made the choices they did. Some things are difficult, if not impossible, to come to terms with, for example, how can anyone place more importance on their status in the community than the well-being of their own child? How do they justify honour crimes? I would include rejection and disownment within the sphere of honour crimes, perhaps not as seen within a legalistic framework, but they are indeed crimes within a moral and ethical context. I believe that choosing to reject or disown a human being because of a families' misplaced notion of honour is as great an issue as physical violence. This situation can have devastating effects on individuals.

I have had to accept that there is, sadly, the capacity in people to believe that a person is 'bad' or 'wrong' if they do not conform. In honour-based cultures, shaming the family and community by what is considered to be selfish behaviour can make you that 'tarnished' person. In order for the affected family to be able to hold their heads up both at home and in public, as well as for them to cope with and find closure or resolution to the matter, it seems that a process of disassociation, or disownment, has to happen. However, I also think that these families believe that the choice to be disowned is made by the victim, since they would be well aware of the consequences of not conforming. The rejection is so much harder to bear when you are told by your family that you have shamed them in other people's eyes. It is also somewhat ironic that the perpetrator is often encouraged and rewarded and receives support for the action of disownment, both by the immediate family and also the individual's community. My exclusion from the framework of community life and unacceptability is a sharp reminder of the injustice of this.

Men and women are rejected because of their life choices, for instance wanting an education or to pursue a career, having a girl or boyfriend that they have met inside or outside their communities or even, for young women, such simple acts as wearing lipstick, cutting their hair, wearing 'unsuitable' clothes, seeking individual independence which should be an opportunity, if not a right for any human being. I remember when being allowed out of the house alone as a young adult was unheard of.

I felt like the 'black sheep' of the family, the one who was different, and being different was not acceptable in my family. When children in local authority care are treated with respect for their differences rather than criticised for them, they form better relationships and feel that they are accepted by their carers and peers because they are understood. I am now clear that as a child, it was the responsibility of my family to care for me despite my difference, as any other family might be expected to do, as I would do with my own children. I do not believe that my difference was an offence as far as any human being would be concerned. My family reminded me of my difference in the negative aspects of my colour, size, intelligence, ability, worth, and so forth. Whether this was knowingly or not, I faced ridicule from them. I know that they could not fail to own this, in the silent moments of their thoughts and reflection.

I am also clear that I was subject not only to emotional and physical abuse, but also neglect. I was powerless to defend myself in the face of clear lack of concern and care. I also understand that families sometimes don't have the ability to manage each others' needs. I know that I may well be the victim of my family's circumstances, that I was the scapegoat for the others' problems, possibly so that they could cope with weaknesses in the family. Despite all these things and the impact on me and my present family, I can say that we have built our lives on strength and hope. I have had to think about what is best for my own children and how I should treat them. I have tried to do this with the respect and love that I believe they deserve; but only they can validate and speak about this.

Many post-disownment experiences can be understood in the context of cultural norms and expectations but many are simply due to the significant losses that are suffered. When I first left home, the thing I remember most vividly is the first night I spent at the teacher's home, lying in a strange bed with a whirlwind of emotions swirling round inside me. I closed my eyes and tried to sleep, but the deep and strange feeling of separation from those I knew and loved, and being in this unfamiliar new space, made sleep impossible. I had never felt so alone. I did not realise how much I would miss being at home with my family, falling asleep with the familiar voices of my parents in the background; consciously or unconsciously, this was such an important part of my being, because it was all I had ever known. I never felt that same feeling again, of belonging to a family. Even though my experiences had been so difficult within the family and I really could no longer cope with the level of rejection, I still felt the need to belong. Most victims or survivors of honour-based disownment that I have met have had loving families and desperately want them back, and struggle more than anything with this loss. Although I missed my family too, I was never assured or given the chance to know them intimately. I have spent a large part of my time away from my birth family trying to understand why they could not reach out to me when I extended a hand to them. Although I have not fully recovered from this, at least understanding my reaction in the context of loss has helped me to move on at some levels. Moving on from the loss of your family is no easy thing for anyone faced with this situation. Victims often say that they lost everything overnight.

Other familiar things that I have shared with victims and survivors alike include special days such as our birthdays, and how we cope with these events which should be a cause for celebration but which are sometimes so painful; also remembering our parents' birthdays, and those of our siblings and their children. These are times when we feel most lonely, shut out from the normal celebrations of life. We feel exposed because we are reminded of our lack of belonging. Christmas is a hard time too, as it is when families come together. I know from my work with children in foster care and adoptive homes that these special times can cause unsettled emotions, and in adults too. I recall being sad, angry and distracted all at the same time, often having to fight off thoughts of the family and the failed reunions of the past. Diwali was a difficult time too, but over the years this has become less important to me, despite keeping the festival alive with my new family. I know now that time can heal, but it can also take a very long time to do so.

Survivors can go on to lead fulfilling and successful lives, but as I discovered when I found myself in front of Ambi at the supermarket that day, the past never really goes away. Confronting it directly can set you back by months or years in some cases. Ambi's final contact with me brought closure, but even now, when I wash my hands I look at them and see hers. For a long time I could not cook Asian food as it reminded me too much of home. We are reminded about our situation by the questions we can't answer on the medical form which ask if anyone in your family has suffered from heart disease or hypertension, how your parents died, when your mother and sisters had the menopause. We are constantly faced with difficult questions by well-meaning people about our family situation, what our siblings do for a living, how many nephews and nieces we have. It is yet another reminder of what could have been. This does not mean that we have not moved on, but that there are scars which take time to heal.

Many survivors express this as feeling like the 'walking dead', especially when they first leave home. I remember the loneliness of this time, before I met my husband, feeling that I did not deserve to be happy. Accepting that I deserved to be alone. The guilt is never far away – the guilt of enjoying things without family or allowing yourself to do something that your family would not approve of. Not having their blessing for your marriage and children. It is not a feeling of elation when you leave home, more one of relief that you have been released from something you can no longer deal with.

In many ways these experiences are more pronounced for Asian men and women from traditional backgrounds; because of the upbringing we have had, our original framework for living was centred around joint decisions about such things as shopping, visiting people and routines which are controlled by others' needs within a household. We were raised to think of what our mother and father and community expected us to do, without question and without being asked. Doing something for yourself was considered selfish, especially from a religious point of view. There were many good things about our culture and religion that I learnt with my family that I still hold on to now, although most of these are things have meaning for any family or group of people who live together. However, the framework of the life that my family led was defined by people who belonged to a particular clan and there was a responsibility involved in being part of this; obedience was necessary to uphold the traditions, morals and values of that community. These had many times the value of an individual's happiness and well-being. I realise too that my identity as an Asian woman was tied up with my birth family and their racial and linguistic origins, the positive aspects of culture and traditions, and that this was the reason why I still sought to identify with them when I left home and the years that ensued, because the isolation of living and finding my identity in Britain was much harder. This is another reason why it has taken me so long to be where I am now. But I have accepted the changes in my new life now and no longer feel the guilt that I initially felt about making independent choices.

Help With The Healing Process

O ver the years I have found that many different paths can lead to healing. The following are some of the experiences I have had which have been very helpful to me and which I hope will help others:

1. 'Know When You've Done All You Can'

Many survivors' deepest wish is to be reunited with their family. I often think that it can be very difficult if this possibility is not explored fully, as the person disowned needs to be convinced that they have done everything that they could to reconcile before they can move on. Even if this is just finding the space to talk through the dilemma with someone, it is better than drawing a line under the victim's loss before they are ready to do so. My hope is that families would seek help to reconnect with the victim that they have disowned if approached but sadly, many do not.

Of course it has to be up to the victim if they want support in contacting their family, but if they do, a safe and risk-assessed process should first be worked out and the implications seriously considered; the approach also has to be well-timed.

For me, the seeking for resolution went on for many years; my family's response was not forthcoming, despite the efforts on my part. I now believe that it is important for survivors to realise that there comes a point when they must accept that there is nothing more they can do to bring their families back, and that this is essential for their full recovery. Moving on becomes impossible if you are always hanging on to false hope.

2.   'Taking Control'

Over the years I often thought of how I might find acceptance with my family, or if it was even possible me to do this. I never had any confidence on this matter as I had no lead from my family as to what, if anything, would be acceptable. Ambi told me that her husband had said that the only way of redeeming myself would be for me to give up my husband. I understand now that for many people, 'redeeming' means 'compliance'. Girls tell me that if they consented to an arranged marriage they would be accepted back in the family, but some can't understand why their family will not see them otherwise. Many more feel guilty and blame themselves for their disownment because their family values still impact on them. I also believe that placing conditions such as leaving my husband would have allowed the control to be placed back with them. Taking control of one's own life is another way to help survivors heal.

I realised when my children were born that I needed not only to be in control of my own destiny but was responsible for theirs as well. With the help of my faith and thinking positively rather than negatively about the situation, I began to see that things could get better. It would have been all too easy to allow myself to slip into further depression and have false hopes, but I now believe that taking control of your life is the best way to move things on.

3.   Rwanda

I found peace in Rwanda. Seeing others less fortunate than myself, people suffering to maintain a basic existence and yet still embracing life, being willing to help others and having faith, has been an inspiration. Yet, Rwanda was a place at one time where there was nothing but discord, the extreme of all the horrors that we could ever imagine. The loss of family left so many struggling and trying to make sense of what life was all about, and yet they carry on and help others to do the same. I have been given many more chances to pick myself up than my friends in Rwanda. My experience comes nowhere close to theirs. The learning from this is that we can always look at those less fortunate than ourselves to arrive in a better place.

4.   <u>Work</u>

My social work has kept me thinking realistically about life. I am no different to the next person I meet and I am also fortunate to have been able to know so many people, from so many walks of life and in so many different circumstances. These lives have changed me and continue to change me, I hope for the better. The colleagues with whom I have worked have meant a great deal to me and will continue to long after I have retired.

5.   <u>Support</u>

I had counselling, and a very understanding GP to whom I am forever grateful. She listened to me when I needed this the most, and she helped me trust my feelings. I am fortunate to have seen that good care can be provided by doctors where there is a willingness to understand the cause and treat at the same time.

I have had the support of Jasvinder Sanghera and Karma Nirvana, in fact, of many good friends – they know who they are. These things have meant a great deal to me and my well-being. We have to take a risk in finding people we can trust, and must not be afraid to ask for help.

MixTogether, my online community, and the people that I have been so fortunate to meet over the last five years or more have also sustained me, and helped me not lose sight of the possibilities for change. I hope this change will be for the better for those who do not want to be linked to an inappropriate match for marriage or life partner, or who cannot deal with the idea that they will be disowned if they don't conform to the pressure from their families. I believe MixTogether is a great support for those who have been disowned, and not least, for those who want help to enable them to reconnect and engage with their families. I have been aware that many of those joining MixTogether have done so not only due to their mixed relationship, but because they need to speak about the dynamic of cultural and traditional expectations on them, positive and negative, defining for themselves how they fit with these ideals, rather than having it placed on them as a restriction. All this has helped me to understand that what I went through with my family is not so different from many others' experiences. This affirmation provides strength and support to many. MixTogether is a dynamic and positive organisation dedicated to its members, welcoming new people to this incredible online community. The learning here is that we live in an amazing time where information is increasingly accessible online, and that many need not be isolated, living without answers to their questions about seeking a better future.

6.   Writing

Another thing that has helped me to heal is writing. I have always written, never felt daunted or particularly worried that I might make mistakes, as this was one way for me to express how I felt, starting with long letters that I would write to friends. I wrote to

Ambi, after the incident with her in the supermarket, twenty one years after she had last seen or spoken with me. I wrote many pages, asking the questions that I had never received an answer to, saying the things that I felt, the anger that I felt had never had a channel – not anger at her, but anger at the situation in which we were as a family. I also wrote asking for her reasons for shunning me, knowing that she may well not be able to give me the truth that I fantasised about, still believing that somehow I would receive it, with honesty. Why did I do this? Because the yearning for such answers is so strong in the face of rejection. In addition however, it was a powerful thing to do, to speak up in the face of rejection, to let go of my silence.

I went on to write what I call my 'letters of healing' after this letter to Ambi, but this time I had no one to send them to: I wrote them anyway, powerful and yes, emotional letters that helped me to say how I had felt about each relationship and what I understood of each member of my family's situation. These letters to my Mamaji, Papaji, Dev, Jay, Noor, and not least Ambi, all helped me to put closure to the situation. I asked Philip to write a letter to my family, which was done with great dignity and strength by him, about what he had felt and witnessed. As I wrote, I felt the tears come until I was unable to see the page, but wiped my face and wrote with strength, until the burden of all guilt, fear, sadness, anger and disappointment fell from my shoulders. Over time, this too gave me and Philip a way to move on. I hope that this way of doing things might help others when they need to get closure if, God forbid, their families no longer want to know them.

When I first left home, I could not believe how differently I had experienced life from those around me. I always knew at school and Sixth Form college that things were different for Asian boys and girls; at nursing college I saw these differences again, and this new life was something that I was not prepared for. I saw for the first time the love of a family and how my friends' parents cared for them. These examples seemed a world away from where I had been. I always knew that I wanted to write about all this, and that someday I would. As the years have gone by, especially after Rwanda where I searched for a way to move on, this has become a real project for me, especially if it helps others like myself. The survivors who have been silenced are the important ones to think about and speak up for.

My first encouragement to write came from Philip and Mike, our friend, who read some of my early ideas for a book. At this point, I wanted to self-publish as it did not matter to me how I did it so long as I could get my story out there for others, hoping that somehow it might help them to tell theirs. Mike said that he thought what he had read was publishable, and encouraged me to keep writing. For the first time I felt some hope. I had a lot of questions and wasn't sure that I could do it. I then thought about this and realised that no one had spoken about disownment in the detail that was needed, particularly about the aftermath. I felt all this was important for others as much for myself and my now family.

7.   Dreams

I would often have bad dreams; these affected me, but I have learnt much from them. I realise that my dreams have been playing out the many memories and experiences of the past. It has been rare for me not to dream of my family but even now, I don't see this as harmful, rather that much healing has taken place over time, and that even nightmares can be put into perspective. For many years, I had dreams of my family's faces in various situations although they never spoke to me; but on two occasions that I recall, I had vivid dreams where my parents came to me at different times and reassured me of their acceptance of my husband and family; these visitations mean a great deal to me, and I believe that they were sent to me at these times for a purpose. I have learnt therefore to keep the good dreams with me. These too are a healing. Again, many survivors talk with me about dreams of their family.

8.   'Managing Things'

As a result of my experiences, I have become a person of routine. I like to know where I am and manage life by doing things in a carefully measured way. This structure has worked for me, and over the years has helped me to shape my life. Survival skills are important, but the skills needed to undergo the emotional journey are even more so, and much harder to acquire. For many years, any bullying at work would affect me very deeply, understandably, but I began to handle these things in a much better way than I had before. It is tough for Asian women who are trying to deal with issues such as this, as well as handling their isolation without family and also facing discrimination and other challenges from the wider society. Learning to manage these situations well is essential but by doing so, one gains the strength to speak out about things that are not right.

There have been other areas of healing. Much healing has come from my faith in God and my love of Philip and the children, a family that I realise I was so fortunate to have.

My experiences and those of victims and survivors known to me have also helped me to reflect on the psychological impact for those disowned and realise that hearing these accounts can support others through these traumatic changes time and time again. I understand that this type of dialogue can enable a victim to affirm that they are not going crazy.

The Future

hil and I hoped that by sharing our situation, we could help people to understand others like ourselves in the community, those who have made the choice to marry a partner from a different race or background to themselves. Also the positive aspects of these relationships are not discussed enough, yet to us they represent the 'community cohesion' that is spoken about so much in this country. I now see many mixed couples who are proud of both sides of their heritage but many families still don't accept this, and these attitudes need to change. The fear of change is real for many people who feel threatened that their religion and culture will be weakened, but I would argue that culture has always seen transformation and movement and for much longer than we believe – and it will continue to evolve. We know from research that in twenty five years' time, the main ethnic group in Britain will be in the category of 'Mixed Race'. There is a large increase in the number of Asian women who are choosing to have white partners (and more white men choosing Asian partners) in the UK and that is certainly our experience on MixTogether. This is something that we must recognise, not just in this country but increasingly throughout the rest of the world. Change is not to be feared when we realise how much richer life is as a result of cultural diversity. Even so, disownment is still a widespread problem in some communities.

I look back and believe that I took this journey for a reason. I have reflected on my experience and no longer feel guilty about saying how it was for me with my family. It has been important for me to tell the story of my own healing and I hope that this will empower others to speak out about what happened to them. The purpose of this is so that we can begin to make the changes necessary through talking, openly and honestly, without being reminded of 'cultural sensitivity' or 'political correctness', and so that everyone, from the individuals affected to the Government, can begin to address and support these issues.

Currently, when people come to the MixTogether forum asking for help with potential family disownment issues, there are very few places where we can send them to get practical support or appropriate counselling. The forum provides a wealth of advice based on members' own experiences: often, listening and sharing is an immense help. People who want to escape abusive situations can be referred to organisations such as the police, Karma Nirvana, and other forced marriage agencies such as the freedom charity, Southall Black Sisters. Many others have become much more aware of the issues of honour and shame in the South Asian community and the physical danger a woman can be in if she does not conform. Yet despite the new laws and voluntary agencies which deal with forced marriages, society has not understood or taken on board the services required to work with individuals who are victims of disownment. I believe that there are hundreds, maybe thousands of cases like mine, but there is little practical help out there and none that deals directly with the problems we face, perhaps because they are rarely aired in public. We have to address this rather than defend the existing situation: I believe that the fear of 'interfering' in cultural issues only serves to maintain the restrictive traditional cultures of communities and ignores the fact that these practices actually take away peoples' rights to make their own life choices and have family support. In fact, ill-considered 'political correctness' can cost lives.

Disownment and rejection are crimes that are not recognised by wider societies because the so-called 'shame' of the victim must be internalised in honour-based cultures, and this prevents the victim from openly sharing their experiences. Sometimes this is made more difficult because of the lack of understanding about the plight of the victim. Victims can be given inappropriate messages about the need for 'cultural sensitivity' and 'political correctness' in society, preventing them from receiving the real empathy and warmth they need to feel as survivors.

The plight of the victim in this situation is rarely recognised if at all in services within our social care framework, for example in the provision of confidentially sensitive support such as counselling and psychotherapy. There is no visible, recognised project or resource that acknowledges how victims' needs will be met. Victims rarely have anyone to turn to and are often left vulnerable in a new community. Survivors may take many years to recover, if ever. Stories of women who have committed suicide are not uncommon. The suicide rate for Asian women is three times the national average in Britain alone. Mental health problems are also much higher in the same demographic group; big issues are anxiety and depression, in men as well as women, which often go unrecognised for years.

Few people fully understand the trauma of the loss of family and the long-term effects it has, even if the survivors make friends and go on to marry. I am fortunate to have been able to build a life without the love and support that you might expect from family, but this is not always the case for others. As a social worker, over the years I have seen children, men and women deeply affected by the lack of understanding from their families: the suffering is terrible to watch and is a huge challenge to professionals and other services alike. I believe that choosing one's own life partner is a basic human right. I am not against arranged marriages as there is evidence that these can work out well where the right match and support is provided. But we also know that coercion to marry someone off against their will can eventually lead to suicide. Disownment also brings feelings of despair.

In law, the 'right to a family life' is applied in many cases where this – family life – is denied, but there is no law that says your family cannot disown you for so-called 'shaming' or 'honour crimes'. I believe that those who have been disowned and cut off by their relatives are also denied one of the most important supports in life, as are their children. Whilst there are laws covering violence and forced marriage, this very human need for family is far from the minds of many, ignored and not yet understood for what it is by the Government and many national agencies. There is little funding available to help people like these rebuild their lives from scratch. The issue is well-known to Asian women's projects which have campaigned for justice for those affected by honour-based crimes; even so, risk and violence are given a greater voice than the effects of disownment and the aftermath of these events on peoples' lives, especially the difficulties of rehabilitation into a new community and the teaching of basic life skills. Appropriate counselling is needed much earlier in the process of rejected individuals to give them a better chance of survival and possibly of being reunited with their families. It is also important to realise that the law does not protect disowned people in terms of their inheritance, or give them the right to learn about the death of parents or other close relatives. I was not informed of my mother's death nor of my father's will. How many more are there out there who are in this situation?

Through the internet, the MixTogether community has made a start, providing support without judgement and regardless of an individual's race, religion, or caste. As some of the stories on the MT forum show, it is possible to see the positive side of mixed relationships despite these differences. It makes me very happy to read successful stories such as Solome's and Leena's, which show that family reconciliation and integration is possible to achieve with the right support and attitude. My work with MT continues, helping mixed couples address the issues of disownment, guiding people through the minefield of family rejection and helping them build meaningful lives and relationships for themselves. It is an area I want to explore further and bring to the attention of the wider public. We started to organise more as a group when we became a charity in 2011. The efforts of our work are now paying off, with members volunteering to help us to organise ourselves. We still have MT meet-ups regularly, both as a committee and with forum members as a social group. These are something I look forward to, as the amazing positive identity of each member and the energy of the group is rarely forgotten by anyone who has attended. We can't get enough time with each other at these meet-ups and when the time comes to leave, no one can quite bring themselves to go, hanging around at the door for the last few words.

The forum has expanded on a wide variety of subjects which are of interest to individuals and mixed couples wanting to explore the issue of honour and how this concept is seen in many Asian families, in particular in relation to marriage and the right to choose who you want to share your future with. Questions are asked about the raising of children of mixed heritage, especially from Asian / white, Asian / black or Asian / other backgrounds; these are addressed through the experiences of couples who give their free time generously and share the reasons for the success they have had as well as the difficulties they still face. The stories on the forum are clear evidence that widespread acceptance of mixed relationships and a right to family life are still a long way off. We cannot afford to deny that these problems exist, but I believe that over the years the extent of these issues will eventually be known and that the research, support and funding that is needed in this area will be provided.

Final Conclusion

One thing I am certain of is that if I had found help sooner, I may not have spent so many years of my life in isolation. If there had been a website where I could have found help and advice from people who understood, because they had been through the same things as me and had made it through to the other side, if there had been clear advice on where to go for professional, legal, medical, financial and spiritual help, and someone who I could speak with on how to reconnect with family, I wonder how different my life might have been. I hope that by writing this book, I am not misinterpreted, as speaking out about this subject is seen by some as politically incorrect because it undermines Asian cultures. This is not my intention: this book is written based on my experiences and validates those of others. I have indeed known many good families, Asian and otherwise, and have seen where 'family' can work. I have been fortunate to know children who have grown up and said that their families have loved them and cared well for them, and that they would be nowhere without the support these families provide. I am heartened and encouraged to know that this is happening, and want to be part of the drive to support anything that keeps families together.

I am from the first generation of people from the Indian subcontinent. I am aware of the changes that have taken place since my teenage years, however I continue to see many of my generation afraid to allow the freedoms that their children need to have to move on and live guilt-free in society.

Just as important are the politicians and influential figures who are aware of these issues and challenges and not ashamed to allow this debate. It is integral to the healthy functioning of diverse communities, yet we skirt around the edges of these issues under the illusion of the preservation of and respect for culture without realising that disownment or fear of this affects a greater number of people than previously thought. The debate is already present in the forced marriage arena.

As my story reaches its conclusion, I can look back from a safe distance and see the learning that has taken place. It was not until I reached my late forties and early fifties that I accepted that there was no longer any point in hoping that I and my birth family would be reunited, or even that my children would be included in their lives. I realise that family is not easily forgotten and that it is painful to be apart from them; even those who are adopted and have never known their families often wonder if one day they will bump into someone who is related to them, usually fantasising about a happy reunion. It took me a long time to deal with the pain of knowing that it was not just me who had been disowned, but in a sense Philip and my children too, and that I was the cause of this. But I have stopped looking back now; memories soften as the years go by, and I am able to place them where they need to be in my mind. When I returned from Rwanda, I knew I had to look forward, count my blessings and take strength from people who had survived far worse than me. I knew what it was like to go through the turmoil of family rejection and disownment, to be torn in two trying to work out what was the right course of action, constantly asking myself if I had done the right thing. I believe I did the best I could and even if I have lost hope of ever being close to my siblings again, at least I have the hope that by sharing my story, some good will have come out of my life. If I can help just one person turn a life of misery into a life of happiness and keep their family bonds, then it will have been worthwhile.

Acknowledgements

Loving thanks to Philip for helping me bring through my story, which is also our story. For his patience over the many months of my writing, and for providing me with the quiet house and the time to reflect, as well as for crying the tears together. To my children, who have always believed in me and supported me through this. Thank you to Muriel, my mother-in-law, for her encouragement and kindness. To my parents, whose lives inspired me, despite everything, and for sharing their world and stories.

I am indebted to my friend Carly for her amazing help and patience with structure and amendments, and to Hardev for typing my first manuscript. To the many survivors who have touched my life, including Leena, Surinder, Solome and Bal, for their stories. To the MixTogether gang, who have shared and believed in my story over the years and become my online family and community, including Ashley, Roopa, Balbir, Jag, Naz, Bal, Pinky, Elizabeth, Maxine, Sonny, Bhav, Rahilla, Jorge, Nelly, Jasmine, and many other brave people, too numerous to mention whom I have had the honour to know.

To my friend John Rushton for being there for me over the years with the help and advice that I have always valued. Thank you to Bobby and Margaret for their reading and comments, to all the other numerous readers including Carly's mates, Pastor Alcot Walker, and not least Zaq.

Thank you to those from forced marriage agencies and other organisations who gave encouragement and support, and a special thanks to Jasvinder Sanghera from Karma Nirvana, for friendship, support, encouragement and shared faith.

Thank you to those at Church, who encouraged and supported me, for being the 'other family' that you have become.

To Nassim, my colleague, for our 'talks', her encouragement and feedback. To Sheila, Monica and Debbie for their love, friendship and laughter.

Thank you Dieudonné for allowing me to share your story: you are a VIP. Thank you Jemrose for allowing me the experience in Rwanda that brought me through, and for the support and love you have shown for my family.

Thank you to the Children in Care Council who have been a source of inspiration to me. To my foster carers and the children who gave me inspiration and helped me realise that friends can be family.

Thank you to my GP, Dr Lott, and to all those at the surgery for being the constant help and support that I have needed.

Thank you to Alnur Dhanani who has supported me with the book and the vision to get the story to those who have been disowned. I am grateful for Alnur's time to read the book and speak to me about the issues that I have raised and his hope that others might find support in reading its pages.

Last but not least, to my publisher Chris Day for his kindness, understanding and skill in helping me to bring my story to book form and supporting my vision.

www.simranslink.org

This is the website that Simran has set up to link those who have been disowned, or fear that they may be disowned because of the misplaced notion of honour and shame.